The Motley Fool's
GUIDE TO

COUPLES & CASH

how to handle
money *with your*
honey

DAYANA YOCHIM

FOREWORD BY DAVID GARDNER

Published by The Motley Fool, Inc., 123 North Pitt Street,
Alexandria, Virginia, 22314, USA

10 9 8 7 6 5 4 3 2

ISBN 1-892547-27-9

Printed in the United States of America
Body set in ITC Veljovic 11/15. Titling set in Futura and Veljovic.

Distributed by Publishers Group West

Cover design by Richard Engdahl
Interior Design by Pneuma Books, LLC
For more information, visit www.pneumabooks.com

Printed by United Book Press, Inc.

1966

The Motley Fool

The Motley Fool's mission is to educate, amuse, and enrich. Begun as a newsletter serving 60 readers in August of 1994, the Fool now reaches millions of people each month and is a leading provider of financial education and independent advice. It serves to help people achieve financial independence across a wide variety of online and offline media channels, including its award-winning website at www.Fool.com, its best-selling Simon & Schuster and self-published books, a nationally syndicated weekly newspaper column carried by more than 200 publications, and "The Motley Fool Radio Show," a joint venture with NPR.

WHAT IS FOOLISHNESS?

Keep in mind as you read this book that, to us, "Foolish" is a positive adjective. The Motley Fool takes its name from Shakespeare. In Elizabethan drama, the Fool is often the only one who can tell the king the truth without losing his head—literally. We Fools aim to tell you the truth, too—that you can learn enough about money and investing to build a secure financial future for yourself. To learn more about The Motley Fool, drop by our website at www.Fool.com or on America Online at keyword: FOOL.

About the Author

Dayana Yochim comes from a long line of teachers, which made her a natural to become the Principal of the Fool's School when she joined The Motley Fool in 1997. As a writer, she de-mystifies investing basics—from annual reports to zero-coupon bonds and brings Folly to all areas of consumer finance, including insurance, home buying, credit cards, car leases, IRAs, and brokerages. Her musings can be found on Fool.com, in the Motley Fool's syndicated newspaper column, in *The Motley Fool Personal Finance Workbook,* as well as on television, radio, and in magazines.

Ms. Yochim was born, raised, and schooled in Lawrence, Kan., earning her degree in magazine and newspaper journalism at the University of Kansas. She spent six years writing for business trade publications in Kansas City and New York before becoming the editor of *Worth* magazine's online edition and then finally taking the leap into Fooldom.

Acknowledgments

Have you ever asked a complete stranger to tell you the biggest money secret they've kept from their spouse? I have. And the answer I got was straightforward, unedited, and educational. On the following pages, family, colleagues, friends, friends of friends, and parents of friends thoughtfully reveal how money works in their relationships—responding to all kinds of probing questions most of us pay a therapist good money to draw out.

This kind honesty from the couples allowed me to prod their secret financial lives and made this book possible. To them, I am indebted and have agreed to misspell all of their names (e.g., "Robhert" becomes "Robert"). But I am most appreciative of the Fool couples who contributed their words and ideas to the first iteration of this long-term project, making it compelling enough to warrant a print version. And especially to Elizabeth and Robhert, er, I mean "Robert" Brokamp—my friends, colleagues, fellow dancers, and the original Foolish couple whose *Couple's Manifesto* serves as the foundation for this line of content.

Additional thanks to the Fool publishing team: Alissa Territo and Jonathan Mudd, for seeing this book to its completion; Jackie Ross, for her lightning speed and eagle-eye editing; and Richard Engdahl, for his artistic flourishes. To David and Tom Gardner, for creating a forum where few topics are taboo—least of all love and money—and having an office where I'm allowed to bring my dog, Poesy, to work.

*To my Mom and Dad, who provided a house
filled with love, forthright answers about money,
and a workable allowance during my
junior high school years.*

Table of Contents

Foreword

When we started The Motley Fool, we were all about stocks. Our Dad had taught us the stock market; we had invested in it from an early age; we loved stocks; we thought stocks were the surest way to long-term riches (we still do); and we built our website, Fool.com, for stock market investors. You got that?

The Motley Fool = Stocks

Or *did,* once.

But after our first book tour in 1996 for *The Motley Fool Investment Guide,* we figured out that the world of money was a whole lot bigger—and a whole lot more complicated. As adults, we're not just asked to choose investments. No siree! We're asked to finance a new home purchase, *refinance* that purchase, manage different forms of debt, make smart tax decisions, save for college for our children, budget, buy a car, write a will or form an estate trust, teach our kids about money, buy insurance, choose a financial advisor... the list goes on and on.

We realized that truly fulfilling our mission of *helping people make better financial decisions* involved a lot more than just picking stocks. In fact, stocks were only one small piece! So, we made an adjustment to that complex mathematical expression introduced earlier. It became:

The Motley Fool = Stocks + Help With
All Your Other Financial Decisions

...which has taken us from what were once 100,000 members to more than two million, entering 2003. In so doing, we've put our little company on the map as the rarest of land masses: an island of diverse and *independent* financial advice. Meaning, no strings attached. As in, "We're not hoping to take control of your money." It may be the most important move we've ever made.

But something was still missing. You see, all the rousing dinner discussions in the world about the biotechnology sector or the importance of a Roth IRA mean *nothing* if your significant other resents having to balance the checkbook every month. With a worldwide community of Fools to listen to and learn from, we discovered that love and money make a complex cocktail of wants and needs, history and reality—a cocktail spiked with a huge shot of emotion. That deserves some additional thinking, and some new and sometimes unconventional advice.

Well, as it so happened, Fool writer Dayana Yochim had just given a talk about "Couples & Cash" to a sold-out auditorium in Boston, Mass. The audience actually clapped. In fact, the audience clapped more than the audience claps for one of the speeches my brother Tom and I give together. So we realized something.

We realized this idea should be a book, and it should be written by *Dayana* and no other. And indeed, over the course of the past year, she has played reporter, counselor, coach, and even referee with family, friends, coworkers, and complete strangers to learn how money works in their relationships. They were gracious enough to share their feelings and household finances with her, and she, in turn, presents what they taught her to you. Get ready to make *their* experiences count for *your* experience. What a lucky spouse or lover or girlfriend or boyfriend (or whoever it may be) you have!

To recap: To make optimal use of your money in your life—one of the most powerful contributors to happiness—you need to know personal finance and stocks. But even more, you need to be able to see these things in the context of loving human relationships. So, we can now update our formula once more:

> *The Motley Fool = Stocks +*
> *Comprehensive Financial Help +*
> *Relevant Relationship Advice*

High time! And we trust you will have a highly good time zooming through this book!

—David Gardner, co-founder of The Motley Fool
December 2002

Introduction

"If you want to stay married, talk about money."

Ponder that for a moment: If you want to stay happily coupled, talk about your finances. That's pretty sound advice, especially considering it comes from long-time Fool David Braze, who has been married more than 40 years.

Since you and your partner have chosen to be together, you probably already see eye to eye on all of life's moral, material, recreational, and economical issues.

If only.

We don't mean to ruffle anyone's feathers, but we've found that few, if any, twosomes agree on all of life's joint decisions. At the extreme, well, you've heard how it goes. He's a spender; she's a saver. He wants to blow the budget on Bruce Springsteen tickets; she wants to save for a down payment on a home. He's a Montague, and she is—you guessed it—a Capulet.

Even if you are both Capulets, there are ways to strengthen the fiscal "happily ever after" factor in your relationship. If you want it to work, talk about it.

That's the goal of *Couples & Cash*—to help you and your spouse (or live-in or fiancé or life partner or "hot lips") smartly face the inevitable financial tensions that arise in couplehood. If you don't have many financial issues, this guide will help you find ways—together—to make your cash go further for years to come.

All the familiar topics are on parade here—setting goals, developing a budget, deciding who organizes the receipts, investing comfortably for two, and preparing for life's inevitable financial emergencies. On the following pages, you'll learn to:

- Measure your financial union against your financial dreams;

- Set priorities you can both agree on;

- Better track your progress;

- Complete the essential documents you need to have on hand for any of life's curveballs;

- Find the delicate balance between financial independence and togetherness;

- Determine the cost of your dreams—the ones you have for your family and for yourself;

- Approach one partner's risk aversion or daredevil attitude.

We consulted countless couples who shared what works and what doesn't when it comes to jointly managing their finances. They generously allowed us to recount their dirty little money secrets—both the successes and failures—in the hope that they will help other couples better cope with cash. Read how they:

- Deal with one partner's debt load;

- Organize accounts from past jobs and romantic unions;

- Handle bills when salaries are dramatically different;

- Decide when "his," "hers," "ours," and "the dog's" makes sense;

- Turn spending resentment into budgeting teamwork.

In the next eight (Brief! Funny! Really!) chapters, *Couples & Cash* will teach you how to cover all this ground with your better half—even if your special someone would rather clean the gunk off of the roof of the microwave than talk about money. (Don't worry, we provide crib sheets and cleaning tips for the uninterested partner.)

You've probably heard the well-worn statistic that money issues are the No. 1 cause of divorce in the United States.

But who cares? You shouldn't. We sure don't. In fact, that's the last time we'll toss off some downer statistic about money ruining relationships. When it comes to love and money, it doesn't matter what waylays your parents, friends, neighbors, and that lady over in Aisle 4, thumbing through the organic cookbooks. It's about finding what works for you two. Because, gosh darnit, you kids are special!

Without further ado, let's find some Foolish solutions to one of life's stickier money management issues—how to handle money with your honey.

There were many tears (mine) and stormy fights about our money styles in the beginning. I'm the kind of a person who needs a general idea of how much money is in my account. My husband writes down every single expenditure—from parking meters to telephone calls. After about five years of marriage, it dawned on us. We might eat at the same table and sleep in the same bed, but we could *not* coexist in the same checkbook! So, I got my own account.

—*Joan, married to George for 40 years*

Chapter 1

He Spends, She Spends

In this chapter, you and your honey will...

- Learn why money is a loaded topic.
- Find out your "money personality."
- Start chatting about your cash.

YOUR MONEY PERSONALITIES

Are you a spender? Are you wedded to a saver? A coupon clipper? An impulse shopper? A Libra? There are dozens of tools in magazines and online to help identify your and your sweetheart's money behavior and astrological tendencies.

None of those matter here. How you arrange the bills in your wallet and whether or not Venus is in Virgo on the 8th of every month isn't really the issue, either. To successfully merge your money personalities, you each need to understand where you're coming from. Or, less cryptically: Wouldn't it be nice to know why your honey seems to buy every Aerosmith reissue, when he already has the originals—on vinyl, cassette, 8-track, and MP3?

Well, it's not that hard to get to the core of why we make the money decisions we do. It all comes down to your relationship with your mother.

OK, we're only halfway joking. But there's a lot to be said for how money was handled by the adults in our lives in our formative years. And while you can't always draw a straight line from a father's nighttime change-counting regimen to his daughter's checkbook-balancing obsession, there's usually some sort of behavioral connection.

Just to make everyone comfortable, you'll hear real-life couples divulge their innermost money secrets throughout this guide. They freely open up their hearts, their checkbook balances, and their households' closed doors to reveal how they make it work. (Stop thinking what you're thinking. This is a finance book, after all.)

First up are Kristin and Shannon, who have been married for 14 years. They've spent a number of those years considering the familial roadmaps that have affected their financial decisions during marriage. Read on, and feel free to boldly steal from what they have learned as you delve into your own money personalities.

1. The past matters.

"Shannon and I grew up very differently. Unfortunately, it took us a while to realize how much this matters in our relationship—especially when it comes to how we handle money as a couple," Kristin says. You may seem like a match made in heaven in every way, but it's important to acknowledge the individual circumstances of each of your pasts. Assuming that your partner will react the same way as you to a sudden windfall or unexpected expense that drains your savings can lead to agitation and misunderstanding in your relationship.

2. People react to their pasts differently.

"My father worked at Walt Disney World his entire career, and my mom was a homemaker. I never worried that they couldn't pay the bills," she says. "Shannon's parents divorced when he was seven, and his mom was the primary breadwinner." As a result, Kristin is much more of a short-term thinker when it comes to finances. She has faith that everything will work out, long term. Shannon, on the other hand, tends to concentrate on the long-term impact of their money decisions. Ah, how opposites attract.

3. Your "money personality" is as individual as you are.

One tangible result of their different backgrounds is their varying comfort levels with debt and

WHAT'S YOUR FINANCIAL PERSONALITY TYPE?

Are you in denial about your checking account balance, or do you track it down to the last penny? Do you frequently make impulsive, budget-destructive decisions? Do even the simplest money management tasks send you into a tailspin or inspire you to buckle down and spend an evening doing long division?

According to an annual study by the Employee Benefit Research Institute and the American Savings Education Council, the majority of people fall into five financial personality types. Where do you and your honey fall?

Planners: Did you always turn in your term papers a week before they were due? Then you're probably a "planner." When it comes to money, the study found that 23 percent of Americans plan ahead for big purchases.

Savers: Nineteen percent of Americans are cautious enough with their money that unexpected events seldom catch them off guard, financially. If you're a saver, we applaud your Boy Scout-like preparedness.

Impulsives: Did you see the sale at Bloomingdale's? Oops. Sorry 'bout that. Impulsives (24 percent of us) understand the importance of disciplined money management. Unfortunately, impulse buying derails their savings efforts.

Strugglers: Though many strugglers (18 percent) consider themselves disciplined savers, they frequently suffer financial setbacks due to unexpected and costly events.

Deniers: Sadly, 15 percent of Americans dislike financial planning. These deniers choose not to address financial matters at all.

spending. Says Kristin: "We got married really young and moved to New York City." What does that spell? T-r-o-u-b-l-e, with a capital "T"—in other words, serious credit card debt. Because Kristin's parents didn't "believe" in debt, she freaked out about their credit card balances. "I thought we were going to have to hit the streets. Shannon, on the other hand, seemed pretty comfortable with having debt." To him, it was just a way of life—how his family got by when money was tight.

4. **Understanding your partner's money personality helps diffuse money misunderstandings.** It's critical to note that dredging up the past isn't an end, in itself. We know some of you are rolling your eyes and itching to get to the numbers. Hold your horses; we promise we'll take you there! Before you break out the calculator, though, take a step back, just for a moment, and acknowledge that your past does affect your present—mainly in terms of what you value. "Shannon values having a secure retirement plan, whereas I value living our dream lives (the specifics of which change as we mature together)," says Kristin. Again, developing a common language and really taking in what your partner needs is more than half the battle.

WARM UP TIME

Feel relieved after reading about another couple's travails? See, you're not the only one who can turn some-

thing as small as a missing can opener (far left drawer—
always the far left drawer, for crying out loud) into a big
fight about who's better with money.

The more you talk (rationally, please!) about your finances, the richer you'll be. If you're like most couples,
however, you may have tried this "adventure" before
with little success.

We've all been there, done that, and we'd rather not go
back. So we came up with a few exercises to help you
and your Sig-O start talking about money successfully.
In other words, we're here to help you have an amusing
and painless conversation.

LIGHTS! CAMERA! ACTION! WELCOME TO THE FOOLY-WED GAME!

Remember *The Newlywed Game?* We've created the fun,
financial version to stimulate dialogue between you and
your partner. The only things missing are the cardboard
signs for you to smash over your loved-one's head.
Though if you're crafty...

Turn to the Worksheet section starting on page 103. This
is where you'll find your first joint exercise—10 leading
questions that will take only a few minutes to answer.
Don't peek at one another's answers. Comparing your
responses at the end is the fun part.

MAKE SOME MONEY SMALL TALK:
FOUR CONVERSATION STARTERS

Setting the proper foundation for money conversations

is so important—and so difficult. Here are a few warm-up questions for you and your beloved to discuss tonight over dinner.

1. Reminisce about your first date. Who paid? Where did you go? What was the price of a gallon of gas that year?

2. How much loose change does your partner have in his/her possession right now? (The person who guesses the closest gets to keep all the change.)

3. If your partner had $10 to burn, how would s/he spend it?

4. Doesn't your beloved look adorable?

Since we got married, we haven't
had time to sit down and have one big, serious
conversation about money. But we've talked enough
to know that we're generally on the same page. We
both hate credit card debt. We both like to have
a cushion in savings. We like to make sure
the bills are paid before we do anything
else. OK, I spend more money on
clothes than he does, but he
spends on books
and CDs.

—*Aimee, married to Jordan for eight months*

Chapter 2

Getting in the Mood (for a Money Talk)

In this chapter, you and Hot Lips will...
- Gear up for an in-depth financial discussion.
- Develop some reasonable ground rules.
- Improve every money conversation.

THE SUPER BOWL OF MONEY TALKS

Lest you thought the last chapter was a bit too touchy-feely, we'll start this chapter talking about football—the strategizing, the loud clack of ramming shoulder pads, the coach's cracking knuckles, ear-splitting screams, penalty flags, giant Styrofoam cheese hats...

Where are we going with this?

Gearing up for "The Big Talk" is like the Super Bowl, minus the face painting (unless you want to make it

SYLLABUS: THE BIG TALK 101

What will you discuss during your mega-event? Consider the following:

- Your big financial goals.

- Creating a budget you both can live with.

- Where you can cut back on spending.

- What will tempt you to break the budget.

- What the heck they were thinking when they created the XFL.

really interesting). The Big Talk, as we've dubbed it, is the major conversation you'll have with Sweetums as you try to get your financial life on track.

For those of you reaching for the remote control at the mere thought of such a discussion, know that you may only need to have The Big Talk once a year. The rest of your talks will be like playing in the pre-season, without quite so much at stake.

You'll start your financial Super Bowl in Chapter 3, but before you suit up with the big boys, we have some pointers for getting your conversation off to a good start.

PRE-GAME WARM UP

Remember the last time you tried to talk about saving for a house, and you ended up at opposite ends of the apartment calling your respective mothers for support? Or what about that time you tried to bring up writing your wills, and you had to make a hasty retreat to the gym because the topic gave you the heebie-jeebies? Your discussions about money matters don't have to be perfect the first time. No one will give you an "F" if you and your partner lapse into a familiar argument. The point is to make small improvements over time, step by step, until you feel financially healthy as a couple.

But what if you can't get your partner to agree to discuss your finances? You're not alone. One partner is often more interested in finances than the other—or at least more interested in talking about them. This imbalance can lead to frustration on both sides, as the interested party wonders, "Why is s/he so irresponsible?", while the less-interested partner thinks, "What's the big deal? We're doing fine. Pass the salsa."

Getting on the same page long enough to create joint financial goals (which you'll tackle in a few chapters) can be tricky. Realistically, you may never arrive at the ideal shared vision. On the other hand, you and your true love may have already hashed this stuff out and could write a book about clear and open communication. (And if you have, thanks for buying this one anyway!)

"NOT NOW, HONEY—I'VE GOT A HEADACHE"

People use a lot of excuses to avoid talking about money.

One great way to involve a reluctant partner is to relate goal setting and saving to something s/he cares about.

Consider how Robert (a "saver") inspired his wife, Elizabeth, (a "dreamer") to get in the mood. Elizabeth explains: "I've been itching to plan our next mega-vacation. Until our last financial talk, Robert resisted my enthusiasm, saying that, as new parents, we should focus on more serious things. To get me excited about budgeting (blah!) and saving receipts (ick!), he conceded that we just might be able to save toward another European trip, albeit a few years off. *Voilà!* I am *all about* budgeting now."

Consider the goodies that excite you and your loved one. Chances are, some will require a bit of cash to come to fruition. Now you can talk about getting busy—working on your finances, that is.

SETTING THE MOOD

Get a babysitter. Unplug the phone. Dim the lights. Grab *The Best of Barry White* CD set and hit "replay."

Now turn the lights back up so you can both see your Quicken spreadsheets. Here are some pointers for changing the mood and setting so you can have a successful money talk.

- **Resolve to do things differently.** Just because you and your partner have had difficulty with money discussions before doesn't mean you can't make progress now. Bring a dose of optimism along with your resolutions.

- **Think outside the box (and the house).** If you think money conversations have to occur at a table with a calculator while the two of you stare at each other intensely, you may be in an unproductive rut. Change the scenery by getting out to a coffeehouse or your favorite pizza place. There's nothing like public scrutiny to force people to be more civilized.

- **Come armed with understanding.** Blame is a sure-fire way to turn financial conversations sour. Money issues are tangled up with wants, expectations, and, most importantly, dignity and pride. "Mike and I have always approached conversations about money with a healthy respect for each other's wants, no matter how unreasonable they may seem," says Sonia of how she and her husband—newlyweds—keep their conversations in check. "We find that it's a lot easier to talk about money when we just accept each other, and then continue the discussion from there." Keep reminding yourself about your partner's money past, which we discussed in Chapter 1. Why does he hate credit cards? Why is she so reluctant to share accounts? If you understand where your loved one is coming from, it's a lot harder to place blame.

Now you're ready to move on to the ground rules.

THE GROUND RULES

You know how to play nice; now it's time to decide on the rules of the game. It may sound hokey to some of you, but what if there weren't any rules in a football game? What if they just made up rules for the presidential election as they went along? It could mean weeks and weeks of indecision and chaos... Imagine that!

Likewise, you shouldn't go into your discussion without thinking about what's important to each of you, what you want to get out of the conversation, and how you'll deal with problems as they arise. Anticipating problems, and heading them off at the pass, are your first steps toward healthy commingling.

Below are some suggested ground rules to keep your money talks productive. If you're of the eye-rolling persuasion, let us repeat: If you set the right groundwork for your financial conversations, they are more likely to succeed.

- **Agree to try.** It's natural to be skeptical about doing things differently, or of even opening up financial conversations. Be open.

- **Accept equal responsibility for changing your lives.** Creating a better financial future falls on both members of the couple. That means you share the angst, the jobs (balancing the checkbook, filling out spreadsheets, cutting coupons), and the rewards (taking that great vacation or sending your kids to college without completely blowing your retirement savings). Still, as we mentioned earlier, you don't need to split the financial bookkeeping if one partner can't stand it. Accepting equal responsibility means splitting chores in a way you can both live with. Consider how Betsy and Lane, who have been living together for one year, divvied up their responsibilities: "As a financial avoider (Lane) and a wanna-be-on-top-of-it-but-has-the-attention-span-of-a-gnat (me), we've found what works best is to break up the jobs based on interest," Betsy explains. "I usually end up with 90 percent of the financial chores, but Lane has to pick up the slack with other chores, like the dishes."

- **Don't play the blame game.** No fair bringing up outside issues, like the fact that his mother insisted on wearing black to your morning wedding. Sonia and Mike have established a time window in which they can fuss about bone-headed money mistakes: "We discuss financial *faux pas* when they occur, but do not use them for ammunition later," Sonia explains. You can play the blame game with your tone of voice and posture, too, so watch out for those silent accusations in addition to the louder, verbal ones.

- **Be honest.** It won't do you any good to hide expenditures when you're trying to make a joint budget. If you feel the urge to lie, ask yourself: What's going on—what are you afraid of? If you know this is a problem in your relationship, deal with it constructively and creatively—like keeping some money separate in a small account earmarked just for you. Sonia and Mike say: "We have a very healthy 'don't ask, don't tell' policy about menial, everyday items that we might disagree about if they were to become a topic for discussion. I'd feel ridiculous trying to justify why I thought it was reasonable to buy a $7 lip-gloss because I had PMS and needed to indulge myself. Seven dollars isn't worth fighting over—or even discussing." Though they respect each other's privacy about pocket-change purchases, they are open and honest about big purchases and expenditures, and they trust each other to balance out the little indulgences with prudent spending.

- **Be realistic.** Don't schedule a two-hour conversation about money every Sunday if the two of you never even have 15 minutes to sit down. Find small ways to keep one another updated, such as notes on the refrigerator with your weekly bank balance.

- **Take a break if your conversation gets heated and unproductive.** Cool down. Review your list of ground rules. Then set a follow-up date to talk again. And don't use this rule as an excuse to avoid tough subjects.

CHEAT SHEET: THE GROUND RULES

For those of you who don't have time to create your own ground rules from scratch, steal some! Here's a good list to start: Scratch out the ones you don't agree with and add your own. ✂

- Agree to try.

- Accept equal responsibility for changing your lives.

- Don't play the blame game.

- Be honest.

- Be realistic.

- Take a break if your conversation gets heated and unproductive.

✂

FOUR PRE-GAME STEPS

Time to get ready for The Big Game. Drop and give us 20!

OK, two-and-a-half pushups are a pretty good start. After you stretch out, use The Big Talk Prep Worksheet (see pages 106–107) to ink on paper your commitment to a productive and fun money conversation.

1. **Set a date.** Pick out the setting for your money talk. Choose someplace new—maybe a park, your bedroom, or a cozy Italian restaurant. (We discourage talks on roller coasters and at restaurants where they serve any dish that's ignited at your

table.) Or just bring snacks (everyone thinks better with food, especially highly caloric munchies). Then decide on a reward you'd like to share when you're done with your first Big Money Talk.

2. **Prepare for the post-game fallout.** Make an Emergency Relationship Repair Kit. Take a toolbox (or any old box) and place inside items that will help you get over a spat with your spouse. You may want to include coupons for eating out, a pair of movie tickets, some old love letters, a poem, a joke book, or your wedding photo. Plan to fail, and then plan to rebuild.

3. **Set your ground rules.** Feel free to borrow the ground rules listed earlier in the chapter. If you know you and your honey need something totally different, it's time to hash 'em out and write 'em up. To customize your list, consider how you communicate as a couple. Maybe your list is only one item long (i.e., "Don't you dare bring up that bad perm I got in the '80s!" or "Let's not bring up that $50 I blew in one hand at the casino during our honeymoon."). If so, great! Some folks may need a longer list. Whatever your needs, make sure they relate to how you, as a couple, have conversations.

4. **Prepare to scrimmage.** Good work, team. Now that you've agreed on your ground rules, you're ready to tackle The Big Game.

Though we vowed to stick together for richer and for poorer, we figured the former would be much more fun. Over the past few years, we've figured out the way to really increase our net worth is to get the money out of our hands. Through paycheck deductions and automatic transfers from our bank account, we've managed to stay on top of our spending and saving.

—*Robert, married to Elizabeth for three years*

Chapter 3

The State of the Union

In this chapter, you two lovebirds will...

- Pick a starting point for your financial future.
- Record where you currently stand.
- Simplify your financial life.

YOU ARE HERE

Nothing says "I love you" like coming home to a balanced checkbook. Well, some things may say it a bit more romantically, but we don't want to tarry too far from our realm of expertise.

To take it one step further, nothing proves your commitment to successfully managing your finances more than having a solid grasp of where you stand—the current state of your union. How much savings do you have as a couple? What outstanding debts do you have? How close are you to reaching your financial goals?

Consider the power of having a handle on this most fragile of topics—a clear, black-and-white answer to, "Can we afford wall-to-wall Berber carpet in the cat's room?" Just knowing roughly where you stand financially eliminates one of the biggest relationship potholes. No more fights in the checkout line about whether you can afford everything in the shopping cart. You'll have to find something else to bicker about after you read this chapter.

THE GLORY DAYS

Think back to when you were single. Whether that was a year ago or several decades ago, your finances, like much else, were probably a lot less complicated. As long as you had enough cash for the weekend and paid most of the bills, who worried about savings or debt?

However, financial sloppiness is much less appealing for couples with responsibilities than twentysome-things, living it up in group houses and subsisting on Cheetos and Tang. *Much* less appealing. At some point, you need to get your financial house in order. If you're reading this book at the urging of a significant other, let's assume now is that time.

Even if you have been coupled for years, picking today as a starting point in your joint financial journey is a fine idea. This relatively uncomplicated task will provide you and your squeeze with a foundation on which to build a happy lifetime of joint finances.

To begin, you'll need to look at the actual numbers that make up your family balance sheet. Don't feel intimidated. We're just checking:

1. How much you own, and

2. How much you owe.

By writing it down legibly in columns and doing a little addition and subtraction, you will produce a family balance sheet. In fact, we provide a stylish Net Worth Worksheet (see page 110), also known as a balance sheet. And if that worksheet gives you the chills, you can use the Cheat Sheet (see page 108) for a quick snapshot. See? No advanced accounting degree required.

TALLYING YOUR ASSETS

A balance sheet consists of what you *own* and what you *owe* (assets and liabilities, in pointy-headed business terms). We'll begin with the fun part: your assets. Financial software programs, such as Quicken or

Microsoft Money, can be helpful in tracking all bank accounts. But whether you use software, a basic spreadsheet, an abacus, or our worksheet, the point isn't to spend hours tallying up everything you call yours. You just want an approximate number.

To begin, consider dividing up your assets into three broad categories: cash, long-term savings, and fixed assets. Examples of each category are:

1. **Cash:**
   - Checking and savings accounts
   - Cash in brokerage accounts
   - Money market accounts and CDs (certificates of deposit)
   - The big plastic jug filled with spare change you've accumulated since your sophomore year in college

2. **Long-term savings:**
   - IRA and 401(k) balances
   - Stocks, bonds, mutual funds, and other financial assets
   - Exercised stock options
   - Cash value of life insurance

3. **Fixed assets:**
   - Housing (the total value of your home—e.g., what you would get if you sold it)
   - Jewelry
   - Car(s)

A FEW THINGS TO REMEMBER

Accounting for "fixed assets" on your balance sheet can be tricky. Many items that fall under this category, by definition, don't necessarily figure into your financial planning.

Most people consider their homes an important part of their long-term savings, for instance. (And for our purposes, we're using the total value of your home. We'll account for the mortgage later.) But unlike the balance in your savings account, your house is not a liquid asset that can be readily converted to cash. However, housing is frequently an appreciating asset, whereas cars rarely appreciate. As a result, you may choose not to include your car, unless you're thinking of selling it soon.

In addition, some personal property, such as antiques, art, or an occasional piece of jewelry, may appreciate in value. But unless you foresee selling it at some point, there's probably little reason to include it in your net worth. (Hint: We strongly urge you not to list wedding rings under "assets"—unless you want to sleep on the couch tonight.)

Now, simply add up these items (as well as any other items not included above—rental properties, ownership of a business), and *voilà!* You've got your total assets.

LISTING LIABILITIES

Now for the less-fun part of building your balance sheet—looking at everything you *owe*. We'll make one primary distinction between short-term and long-term debts. This is more than just a question of time, however. See if you notice any difference between the two groups we list as examples:

1. **Short-term debt:**
   - Credit card debt
   - Bank loans and lines of credit
   - Charge accounts

2. **Long-term debt:**
   - Mortgage
   - Student debt
   - Car loans

Need a hint? Aside from the term, or length, of the loans, the other difference is that long-term debts preferably represent some form of investment. A mortgage certainly falls in this category, representing an investment in housing, while student debt represents an investment in education and developing work skills. A car loan is borderline, but presumably, you get something out of owning a car. Car loans should share at least one other characteristic of long-term loans—a lower interest rate than your shorter-term debts.

Clearly, not every liability will fit neatly into one of these two categories. Alimony, for example, will most likely be a long-term liability, not an investment—all feelings about ex-spouses aside.

YOUR NET WORTH
And now for the moment of truth: Subtract your liabilities from your assets, and you have your net worth. Ideally, this will be a positive number, and if so, congratulations! Go give your honey a big smooch.

If your number turns out to be negative, don't despair: That may be one reason you're reading this guide. In addition, there are plenty of legitimate reasons for a negative net worth, particularly if you're young and carrying lots of student debt. (Heck, go ahead and smooch your honey if the number's negative, too.)

The important point is that you now know where you stand, financially. That's a *big* accomplishment—one that puts you ahead of the majority of Americans.

In addition, this exercise can give you a peek into your cash flow situation. Compare your cash and short-term debts: Which is larger? You'll get a clearer picture of your day-to-day cash flow in the next few chapters, but the point here is that if your credit card debt is higher than your cash on hand, your balance sheet won't improve in the near future. On the other hand, if you've got more cash than credit card and other debt, you're in good shape to increase your net worth over the long haul, even if you're starting in negative territory.

HIS, HERS, OURS

The balance sheet is only part of your financial couplehood. As you leaf through your brokerage and banking account statements, perhaps you noticed that you have 13 inactive bank accounts between you. Or maybe you found a few uncashed checks from the wedding. And, what the heck—you're still paying for cable TV in a bachelor pad you moved out of sometime in the 1980s?

If you're in the process of combining your financial lives, which can take a while, you may find the two of you have more bank accounts, credit cards, and dusty 401(k)s than you need. Even if you've been together for some time, it's probably been a while since you accounted for all your money.

What a great reason to get organized! (Forgive our enthusiasm, but a little obsessive-compulsive glee does wonders in situations like these.) Let's dig a little deeper and take an organizational and somewhat philosophical audit of your accounts. By taking a closer look at *how* you're managing your checking accounts, credit cards, and savings as a couple, you may find ways to save money and lessen any conflicts that have arisen in your relationship.

CHECKING ACCOUNTS

As you combine finances (or reexamine them, if you've been together for some time), you'll face the age-old question: joint or separate checking accounts? And of course, there's the age-old answer, which is that there is no right answer. Different couples will find that different things work for them.

There are really three options available:
- A joint checking account
- Separate checking accounts
- A joint account and separate accounts

Even if you've already made this decision, it's worth a quick reexamination. Whether you have separate or joint accounts and how you track them could have a significant effect on how you and your partner communicate about money.

JOINT ACCOUNTS

While it may seem natural to open a joint checking account and be done with it (given that togetherness for eternity is about sharing and all), keep in mind that there are advantages and disadvantages to doing so. Don't go hog wild pooling your pennies without giving it a little bit of thought.

Let's begin with some of the advantages of joint accounts:

- **Less paperwork.** One account, one statement—it's a pretty simple setup. A joint account also tends to involve lower maintenance fees (depending on your bank's policies) than two separate accounts.

- **Improved communication.** To keep your records square, you both need to know when one of you spends money for anything more than lunch or a cup of coffee.

- **Easier management of joint expenses.** Paying for children's expenses, for example, is easier since you don't have to coordinate two accounts and figure out who pays for what.

- **Easier access to assets.** A surviving partner doesn't have to wait for a will to be executed to access a joint account. (FYI: We'll be making morbid points like this every so often.)

- **A tangible example of your strong bond.** You sure can't spell "mine" with the letters in "our money." (*"Mone"* is as close as we could get.)

On the other hand, joint accounts have some disadvantages. Let's take a look:

- **Greater potential for error.** After all, how reliably did you balance the checkbook when it was just your account? Now you have to do it for two and may have to work a bit harder to avoid errors.

- **Unequal management.** In order to avoid errors, one person may, willingly or not, become the sole manager of this "joint" account, resulting in a disparity within the relationship and possible resentment. If one person *enjoys* managing the money in a relationship, this may not be a problem. But if someone feels they've had a lot of extra work foisted on them, or, on the other hand, that they have no say or awareness of the family's financial situation, then conflicts arise.

- **No privacy or independence.** A joint account may create tension whenever either spouse engages in frivolous or hobby-related spending.

There will be little room for "fun money." And if you want to buy a gift for your special someone and don't want them to know how little—er, how *tremendously much*—you spent, that will be hard with a joint account (though some couples solve this by having separate credit cards).

- **More trouble for troubled relationships.** To make another romantic point, a joint account can be sticky in a divorce, particularly if one partner feels entitled to more than half of what's in it. And that's not including the possibility that one person could virtually clean out the account and take off to Tahiti without the other's knowledge, should the relationship fall apart.

Of course, separate accounts have their advantages and drawbacks as well, most of them the flip sides of those listed previously. In cases where one or both of you are remarried or have children from a previous relationship, separate accounts are useful for things like alimony and child support.

TWO COUPLES WEIGH IN ON THE "HIS, HERS, OURS" ISSUE
The case for separate accounts:
Sonia and Mike: "Marriage can make you crazy if you feel like you don't even have the autonomy to overspend on makeup every now and then," Sonia says. "Even though we are married, we are still both responsible, independent adults, and it's nice to be treated that way. Maintaining separate accounts prevents us from

TO MERGE OR NOT TO MERGE

That is the question for a lot of couples. Here are a few considerations to help you ponder the age-old dilemma and frightfully overused Shakespearean wordplay:

- **Salary/income levels:** Are your salaries dramatically different, or does only one of you work? If so, the partner bringing home most or all of the money may feel penalized by a joint account, depending on how it's handled. Of course, separate accounts might be even worse in this situation, if a non-working partner is forced to rely on the other for what might amount to an "allowance."

- **Who handles the bills?** With separate accounts, it may not seem difficult to split fixed bills, but what about variable ones? In the case of phone bills, for example, if one of you spends more time on the phone than the other, having one partner cover the bill might be a problem.

- **How do you divide expenses?** Does each of you pay roughly the same dollar amount? Or do you contribute a similar proportion of your take-home pay? This may not make much difference, but it's worth discussing. If you're both paying equal dollar amounts, but one of you earns significantly more than the other, this could be a problem if it leaves one partner with a lot less spending money.

Some of these issues have been mitigated by online account access and personal finance software. Whether you have separate or joint accounts, using these tools can make it much easier to track your finances. Even your bank's 800 number (which enables you to call and get your exact balance) can be helpful.

feeling like we're always looking over each other's shoulder."

She and her husband have switched roles as the bread-winner of the family—one worked while the other was in graduate school. "We have each known what it's like to depend on the other for cash. We've become extremely averse to the idea of an 'allowance' in our relationship. We've avoided this degrading scenario by making sure that whoever is making the money is also paying the bills. Usually this works pretty well, since the non-working party can rely on whatever remains in his/her checking account as spending money. If that fund runs low, the working party just writes the non-working party a check for a lump sum. This allows the non-working party continued autonomy, and we avoid feeling like we have to ask Mom for $20 for the weekend."

The case for joint accounts:

Stephanie and DJ: "Our philosophy about money and our relationship is to always keep the big picture in mind, and to not let the daily grind interfere with that," Stephanie says. That big picture includes a comfortable future where they can continue to use their cash for play and travel. They pool their money into one big pot. Both names are on all accounts (they are not married)—everything from checking and savings to the money market and brokerage accounts. "We don't split bills or bicker about who contributes what," Steph says. "There are times when he contributes more or I contribute more. We are very aware and respectful of each other's contribution, whether it's more or less than the other's—it doesn't matter. We both know we work hard for what we put in. It all comes out in the wash, in the long run."

CREDIT CARDS

How many credit cards do you have? As a couple, do you have more than three or four? If so, why? Are you carrying debt on those cards? How will you pay it off? These are certainly tricky questions, particularly if one partner brought a lot of credit card debt into the relationship.

The Fool has plenty of advice on paying off credit card debt (just head to http://credit.Fool.com). Once your debts are paid off, consider whether you really need more than a few credit cards. You may want one for frequent flier miles, and you may want to consider each having a card in your own name to maintain some independent financial history. Having all accounts in both names won't help either of you establish your own credit history.

Other than those reasons, we don't see the need to haul around a wallet full of plastic.

SAVINGS, IRAS, AND 401(K)S

Moving on from day-to-day cash management, next comes savings. If you and your significant other have had several jobs, then you may have several leftover 401(k)s or other employer-sponsored retirement accounts sitting around. Quick! Look under the couch! (Just kidding.)

More importantly, if you're both working, look at each other's 401(k) plans, assuming they're available at both jobs. Which offers better employer matching? Which has better investing options (such as index funds)? It may be advantageous to pile as much as possible into only one of your work retirement plans and use the other person's salary for additional savings in an IRA or regular brokerage account. (We'll get into the topic of investing for two in more detail later.)

Also, consider any disparities in your current savings for retirement. If one of you has a hefty 401(k), for example, and the other has little or no retirement savings, then you need to discuss whether this creates any issues. Do you both feel you're contributing equally toward retirement? Do you both have some of your retirement assets in your own name? And—to be romantic again—how would these accounts be divided up in a divorce?

Finally, are you and your partner named as beneficiaries on each other's 401(k) and IRA accounts? If you set them up before you got together, presumably not. That's worth changing, of course—particularly if your partner has an ex-spouse currently named as the beneficiary. (We've heard stories, and they ain't pretty!) On pages 121–128, we provide a checklist for your accounts

SHACKING UP

Unmarried couples face many of the same administrative money issues as their matrimonially bound counterparts. While you may not be covered under each other's work insurance plans or eligible for the family discount card at the Korner Kwik-E-Mart, you do have joint decisions to ponder:

1. Who will pay for what? Are you going to pool any of your accounts or split utilities, food, laundry, and dog treats 50/50?

2. Which expenses will be shared and which will be separate? What if one person has more debt than the other? Is that his/her entire responsibility? What about childcare and personal travel?

3. Who will be in charge of paying the bills? Ah, yes—the age-old question rears its head among anyone who shares a phone line, electricity, and a roof. Will you establish one account where you each contribute money toward household bills? Will one person pay the phone bill and the other pick up cable TV?

Regardless of whether your mother is cool with your cohabitation, you need to address these questions.

so you can keep track of beneficiary designations and figure out which ones need updating.

INSURANCE

If you haven't already, check out each other's health plans. As with employer-sponsored retirement plans, one of you may have better coverage than the other. It may be advantageous for one of you to drop coverage through your employer (and perhaps receive higher pay) and apply for coverage under the other's health plan. Just make sure it isn't overly difficult to switch back, in the event that your spouse changes jobs.

THREE WAYS TO SAVE MONEY THROUGH MARRIAGE
Marriage offers love, comfort, and the potential for financial savings. Here are three ways to cash in on couplehood.

1. **Exploit your boss**
   The first place to look for marital savings is your employers. Closely compare your benefit plans for duplication. For example, if your spouse can cover your health insurance, maybe you can opt for other options, such as a cafeteria plan, additional vacation time, supplemental life insurance, or dental coverage.

   Compare 401(k) matching. If one person's employer is more generous, then you may want to max out that person's 401(k) first. See if either employer offers charitable giving, matching, or other benefits for donation.

2. **Exploit your bank**
   Although couples have many different bank account options (a single combined account; two separate accounts; his, hers, and ours), be sure they are linked in the bank's mind so you qualify for lower fees or higher interest rates, which usually

require a minimum deposit across accounts. Most national banks require a $1,000 to $5,000 minimum to relieve you of fees and possibly provide interest-paying checking. (Or just opt for no-fee checking, and put the extra level of money required for interest-paying checking into a brokerage account, where you can buy stocks or, at least, collect interest on a cash money market account.) Also, consider online banks, which often have lower minimums and may be more convenient for bill paying.

3. **Exploit your insurer**
   Car insurers, in particular, want you to be married (almost as much as your parents and smug married friends) and will then discount your rate, especially for young men. Combining auto policies (as well as any other insurance policies—renters, homeowners, and so forth) should get you a discount, since you will become a bigger and better customer to them.

   There are many, many types of insurance, including life, disability, long-term care, health, dental, vision, home, mortgage, and renters insurance. Each has variations in premiums, deductibles, and co-pays. (Get the whole spiel online at http://insurance.Fool.com.) If you haven't updated your policies, make sure they fit your current financial state. Maybe you can afford a higher deductible now and can lower your premiums.

Difficult times hit Texas and our finances in the 1980s, just as we had three kids starting college. The two of us pulled together, cut many expenses, minimized unnecessary expenditures on luxuries, and sold what stock we could to cover the cost of getting the children through to their initial career experience. That was our priority. We're proud of the fact that our four children have seven undergraduate and advanced degrees. Though the cost of those seven degrees was high, we wouldn't have had it any other way.

—*Bob, married to Joan for 44 years*

Chapter 4

Setting Priorities

In this chapter, you and Shmoopy will...
- Identify your top priorities.
- Determine the cost of those dreams.
- Take those first few financial "baby steps."

DAYDREAM BELIEVER

The scene is magical. The table is swathed in brocade silks, nestled close to the private dining room's fireplace. The lighting is perfect. The *foie gras,* succulent. To top it off, you're having a really good hair day.

As your meal winds down, a finely dressed waiter with an impressive French accent approaches. Carrying your rejected Visa, Jacques whispers, *"S'il vous plait,* Madame, it seems zat you're over your credeet leemeet."

Merde.

We all dread such *merde* moments. But they're easily avoidable: It all comes down to setting priorities—a critical step for all couples. Priorities help you decide together what matters most in your relationship. And when the bill comes and it's time to pony up, you're prepared—you've already earmarked the euros for the occasion.

"OUR" DREAMS...

Ideally, you and your Madame/Monsieur Charming will sit down knowing what matters to you: You will tell each other what you really, really want, and then laugh merrily because *you both want the exact same things!*

Or, more realistically, if you're like Duffy and Dan (married for four years), your goal-setting discussions go more like this:

> Duffy: *"Dan—I just updated my three-year plan using my Franklin Covey planner. I have my goals categorized into five major areas: Family, Work, Friends, Community, and Learning. When we work through the list, I will explain some of the subcategories and my footnoting methodology. Do you want to use my template?"*

> Dan: *"Um... I don't write goals. You know that. Do we have to do this again?"*

Clearly, formal goal-setting sessions don't work well in all relationships. But that doesn't mean you shouldn't set goals together. Duffy and Dan told us their goals tend to come out over dinner conversations. You and your significant other will need to find the time and place that works best for your styles. Remember the things you may have learned from conversations earlier in the book, such as your attitudes about money, your past successes handling finances together, and the areas in which you tend to procrastinate.

BIG GOALS

Setting major goals and priorities means identifying the one or two things you really want to strive for—things that keep you excited and motivated. The best goals are the ones you so look forward to that the steps required to achieve them become easier.

Different families will have different big financial goals, based on life stage and lifestyle. Those goals will be deeply intertwined with life decisions that may not be financial, but have big financial implications (such as having a baby, getting married, or moving to a new city). Depending on the stage of your relationship, one of your big goals may be to:

- Buy a home (or a vacation house)
- Get out of debt
- Have/adopt a child
- Live on one salary
- Retire early

- Send a child to private school/summer camp/college
- Start a business
- Get a new car
- Get a new nose and chin
- Change careers
- Take a dream vacation (away from the aforementioned children)
- Go to graduate school (to show off the aforementioned new nose and chin)
- Remodel the kitchen

One common glitch with goal setting is not knowing what you want most. Duffy and Dan thought they wanted a bigger house. When they more closely examined why they wanted to move from their condo, it turned out it was mainly because they didn't like the little kitchen. So they decided to focus on redoing the kitchen—buying remodeling books and looking critically at other kitchens. ("Did you see Stephanie and Josh's beveled-edge Corian countertop?")

Now it's your turn! Together, jot down all the goals that come to mind, using the space provided on page 111. But remember, setting goals means focusing on *one or two priorities* so you can achieve them, and then setting new goals and working your way down the list. If you try to accomplish everything at once, you may end up with nothing.

To narrow down your list, talk through some of the questions below with your partner:

Q: Do you have debt? How important is it to pay off that debt right now? For example, you probably want to pay off credit card debt as soon as possible, but you may choose not to put extra money toward your mortgage. As a general rule of thumb, debts with double-digit interest rates should be paid off before any others.

Q: Are the necessities covered? These could include establishing an emergency fund, fully funding an IRA or 401(k) account, and getting life insurance policies. The reason? Without an emergency fund, for example, an unexpected expense could completely throw your savings plan off course.

Q: What major life events are you expecting in the next three to five years? Is your income likely to change in any big ways—going back to school, changing careers, becoming a stay-at-home parent, retirement?

Once you have more perspective on how your "wish list" matches up with reality, have each partner write down his/her Top 5 list separately, and then compare notes. We offer a worksheet (see page 112) to help you keep track.

PRIORITIES THAT GROW WITH YOUR FAMILY

Mark and Grace have been married nine years, which has included three graduate schools, five jobs, four cities, five living accommodations, one puppy, the addition of three children, and the subtraction of one full-time income. As they explored their financial priorities, they developed a common set of principles about money that has helped guide their decisions. Says Mark: "Explicitly agreeing to a set of high-level principles has really helped us handle our finances." Their three guiding principles are: 1. Live within their annual income; 2. Budget for retirement, college, and charitable giving ahead of all else; and 3. Borrow money only for a mortgage.

When Grace became a stay-at-home mom, the couple had to adjust their priorities accordingly. "We have had to work that into our budget and adjust our lifestyle— meaning living in a smaller and older house, buying used cars, and taking fewer vacations," Mark says. "But we felt the benefits outweighed the material sacrifices."

WHAT'S IT GONNA COST?

Looking over your list, you'll probably notice you have short- and long-term goals. Maybe you want to travel to Bora Bora next year but aren't planning to buy a new house for at least five years, and you don't think you'll retire for another 20 years.

How will you pay for these dreams?

Systematically, that's how. To help keep track of how much you need to save toward each goal, turn to the worksheet on page 113 to calculate costs, right down to monthly (or even per paycheck) amounts.

YOU WANT *WHAT?!*

There's real potential for tempers to flare when setting goals. Why? Many couples disagree about what they *want* versus what they *need,* and who has the right ideas for the financial health of their union.

Don't let *your* conversation disintegrate into heated chaos. In the interest of maintaining some semblance of a mutual financial future, now is not the time to bring up fundamental questions about the relationship. Things like, "We want such different things out of life—what are we doing together, anyway?" shouldn't be uttered during this critical step. Straying off topic and into the deepest, darkest recesses of relationship angst is a sure-fire way to cut off all communication, just when things could start to turn around.

Instead, push yourselves to find common ground. Use the ground rules you established in Chapter 2 to keep your conversation civil. Even if you only agree on one big goal (retiring early sounds good, doesn't it?), you have made progress.

After you identify one mutual goal, agree that each of you can come up with one major goal of your own (within reason). He may want to buy a Jaguar in five years; she may want to attend a writer's conference on the West Coast. Try to support one another's goals, even if your partner wants to work toward something that doesn't interest you.

What if you don't have enough money to save for each goal? Well, you can reduce the cost of your goals—that could mean axing a goal or two from your list, scaling back on a few (a week in the Caribbean instead of a year), or extending the length of time before you expect to achieve some goals.

HOW TO PAY FOR...

Everything. Yup, that's right. If it costs money, then The Motley Fool has suggestions on how best to pay for it. Next time you're faced with a major (or minor) buying decision, stop by www.Fool.com for a few tips:

> Buying a Car—www.Fool.com/car
> Buying a Home—www.Fool.com/house
> College Savings—www.Fool.com/csc
> Retirement—www.Fool.com/retirement
> Insurance—insurance.Fool.com
> Short-Term Savings—savings.Fool.com
> Credit—credit.Fool.com
> Financial Advice—TMFMA.Fool.com
> Tax Help—www.Fool.com/taxes
> Investing—www.Fool.com/school

If we haven't covered a particular spending topic, then someone in our community of more than a million Fools probably has. See what they have to say at boards.Fool.com

Or you can increase the amount you save. How? Funny you should ask. That—not coincidentally—is the subject of our next chapter.

FOUR BABY STEPS TO BIG GOALS

Priorities are probably going to vary greatly from couple to couple (and even between two partners). But whether you're planning to buy a new house or pay for a beveled-edge Corian countertop, you probably won't be able to buy all of it by next pay day. Here are some tactics to help you achieve your goals.

1. **Be specific.** Lay out exactly what you will do differently. For example: "I will increase my 401(k) participation from 5 percent to 10 percent to save for retirement faster."

2. **Be realistic.** You know yourself and your spouse. You know what spending patterns are "must haves" versus "nice to haves." Don't go overboard cutting out all of the "nice to haves," though. Pick a few things to continue to spoil yourself with.

3. **Think "action-oriented."** Goals should make you do something specific: "I will limit shoe shopping to one pair every two months," rather than, "I will buy fewer shoes."

4. **Make your goals known.** Goal-setting theorists (Yes, there are such things!) have long known that people are more likely to meet goals if they have made them public. Tell your friends about your plans. Put goal "check-ins" on your calendar. Use online "nag" services to remind you via email: "Have you paid an extra $100 of your credit card balance this month?"

What saved our marriage?
We each take an allowance out of
our monthly income. We were married
for more than 30 years before we
figured that out. But at
least we figured
it out.

—*Shirley, married to Jerry for 45 years*

Chapter 5

...And Budget Makes Three

In this chapter, you and your better half will...

- Confront your budget demons.
- Get tips from real-life couples.
- Choose from three budgeting approaches.
- Decide how often to review your budget.

THE BIG BAD "B" WORD— BUDGET

When you think of a budget, what comes to mind? Control? Self-denial? Having a dental intern extract an impacted molar?

It's likely that you associate budgeting with boredom, unpleasantness, and futility—just three of the 273 emotions couples tell us they experienced when the topic of accounting for their cash came up in their relationships. Most would rather clean the gunk off the roof of the microwave than sit down and make a budget.

Take comfort in the fact that few people actually put together the kind of budget spreadsheet suggested in all those personal finance tomes. (Although, if you are so inclined, we have written a dandy guide, *The Motley Fool Personal Finance Workbook,* that helps you build a budget bit by bit.) And of those that do, we'd venture to guess that only a small percentage actually follow through.

Still, the idea of budgeting is a really good one. Here's why:

- Tracking your expenses and controlling your money will lead to better decisions. You'll spend less on things that aren't important to you and more on your major goals.

- Finding ways to save just a few dollars a day can pay off, big time, down the road. A 40-year-old who contributes an extra $60 to her Roth IRA each month would have an extra $54,890 at retirement (assuming 8 percent annual growth, a 28 percent tax bracket, and no intervening Armageddon).

- You'll get a realistic idea of your true discretionary income. Knowing that you can spend only $100 eating out each month, you can weigh whether you want to blow it all in one night at a fancy restaurant or spread it out over 37 visits to Taco Bell.

BUDGETS THAT WORK

Have you ever noticed that there's no way to use the letters in the word "frugality" to spell "fun"? The closest we've come is *"frug."* But we all know that budgets can be as fruitless as they are *frug*-less. Even though we *should* make one and stick to it, the reality is that most of us don't.

It may take several months—or years, even—for you and your honey to get into the budgeting groove. And, we'll be honest; most couples have to work on it constantly. But as you catch your stride, you'll find money you didn't know you had (really!) and gain perspective on your finances.

Repeat this Foolish money mantra: The best budget is the budget that works for you. *The best budget is the budget that works for you.* True, a more detailed budget is more accurate. However, every couple must decide whether that detail and accuracy is worth the time and trouble.

We asked couples to share budgeting systems they actually follow. All of the budgets have these things in common. They are:

- **Manageable.** An overly detailed, burdensome budget is doomed to fail. You'll give up on it, and the feeling of failure will leave you worse off than before you started.

- **Linked with rewards.** Come up with ways to reward yourselves for keeping up with your budget.

Dinner out? Posters from the National Gallery of Art? A Liberace Beanie Baby?

- **Fun (sorta).** Watch a video and eat popcorn while you go through receipts.

- **Shared.** Don't expect one partner to do this two-person job.

PAST SPENDING

Before mapping where your money will go, it helps to have an idea of where your money has been. If you make most purchases with credit cards, debit cards, and checks, your job will be easier. If you deal mostly in cash, or you feel you have a general idea of how much you spend monthly on each category, you can estimate past expenditures.

However, as you track expenses to see if you're sticking to your budget, don't be surprised if you discover that your estimates aren't accurate. David tells the story of how he and his wife, Betty Jo (his better half for more than 40 years), tried to create a cash flow statement for their first budget. According to David, "We argued most vehemently about the amounts we were spending in various expense categories." So, for the next 60 days, David and Betty Jo recorded each and every time they opened their wallets.

The result? They were both wrong. "We thought we knew where the money was going, but the truth of the

THE BRIGHTER SIDE OF BUDGETING

It's time for a perspective shift. Though budgeting will never rival a day spent lolling in a hammock (or even three weeks in full-body traction), there's no reason to go into it with a negative frame of mind. Here are a few new ways to think about budgeting:

- **A budget doesn't control you—you control the budget.** You decide on the priorities—what deserves your hard-earned dollars. Yes, it probably means you should curb spending on some unnecessary items. But that's only to fund the really important stuff. You're not just giving up bonbons—you're saving for that house with the wraparound porch and dormer windows.

- **A budget is all about knowledge, not self-denial and stinginess.** Once you've gathered your financial facts, you have the knowledge necessary to make good decisions. The point is not to squeeze the enjoyment out of your life, one dollar at a time; it's to give that saved dollar greater meaning, like, "This gets me $27.50 closer to owning a vintage VW van!"

- **The best budget is the budget that works for you.** Don't abandon the idea of budgeting because you can't do it perfectly, or you don't have enough time to go over piles of receipts and input each one into your financial database. With a little creativity, you and your partner can come up with some quick, easy ways to stay on top of your inflow and outflow.

matter was we didn't," David says. "It took the written record to show us that."

DOING THE DARNED THING

There are many ways to devise a budget. We present three: the Whole-Baked Budget, the Half-Baked Budget, and the Baby Budget. These are just guides; you and your bedmate should design a budget that accounts for your own lifestyle. We present them in detail in the worksheets on pages 113–119.

The Whole-Baked Budget (see pages 118–119) involves tracking all of your expenses for a period of time, and then developing a spreadsheet you can analyze one extremely *frug* evening over mugs of hot chocolate.

If following the trail of every dollar is too daunting, try the Half-Baked approach (see page 117), and boil your budget down to broad categories. Choose two or three of your biggest expense categories (such as food), and break them down in more detail (such as groceries, eating out, lunch, and takeout). This will provide you with enough information to start on the road to budgetary bliss—and may reveal some shocking realizations. ("You spend $30 a month on Skittles?!") Once you've got a grip on the bigger categories, you can gradually become more detailed, as necessary.

If neither of the Baked Budgets is to your liking, we draw your attention to the Baby Budget's top-down approach (see pages 114–115). Essentially, the formula is:

Income − Fixed Expenses *(including savings)*
= Discretionary Money

FRUGAL *V.* WEIRD: A FINE LINE

Philadelphia Inquirer columnist Jeff Brown had no idea what he was in for when he half-jokingly solicited entries for the "First Annual *Philadelphia Inquirer* Cheapskate Contest" at the end of one of his columns.

What followed were more than 300 entries from cheapskates around the country. The winner had to fulfill Brown's criteria: "The top cheapskate entry would have to be eye-opening, clever, and detailed. Most important, like any successful scientific experiment, it would have to be repeatable—something others could emulate."

As Fools on the Living Below Your Means discussion board know (boards.Fool.com), it's hard to pick just one winner. So Brown named winners in several categories, including "Most Questionable, From a Health Standpoint" (Winner: the man who cools his drink cans in the toilet tank); and "Least Valuable, From a Monetary Standpoint" (Winner: the man who extends the life of his turn-signal bulbs by signaling only when there's traffic).

The overall winner: retired Army metallurgist Peter Nowalk, a frugal flosser. He saves $5.06 a year by implementing his home-grown looping method and sterilizing the unused ends for future use. He gets about 14 days out of a 10-inch piece of floss.

Our frugal Fool hats off to you, Mr. Nowalk. We're going to stick to rinsing out Ziploc baggies here at Fool HQ.

With each version, we recommend that you first list the goals you created in Chapter 4. Remember, this is the real purpose of a budget: *to make sure you achieve your goals.*

HOW COUPLES COPE

How do couples actually make the day-to-day hassles of budgeting work in their households? Whatever way they can. Consider these examples.

Use simple math. Duffy and Dan developed a simple method to monitor their spending as they set up their first budget. Worried that they would nitpick over how they spend money, they agreed not to charge anything but essentials, such as gas and groceries.

They were each allowed to spend $100 in cash a week. In Duffy's words, "This was enough that we didn't feel like we were scrimping and eating PB&J all the time, but also small enough that we now think twice about ordering takeout for dinner."

This system is easier for them than monitoring car payments, the mortgage, and electricity bills monthly. Best of all, their simple math method has saved them thousands of dollars.

Make it automatic. Steph has an accounting background and likes the details of bookkeeping. ("Go ahead— call me a freak," she jokes.) So the home accounting has fallen into her lap. To ease the monthly burden, she and her other half, DJ, have set up as many bills as they can on autopayment, so the actual bill paying is minimal. All that remains is balancing the checkbook, which Steph happily (really!) does. "DJ and I rarely bicker about cash. We only ponder the possibilities of how to stay happy and keep the pile growing."

Remain flexible. Tom and Vilis are same-sex partners who have been together for four years. They are typical of couples who meet later in life (early 40s) in one major respect: They are used to financial independence. "Budgeting has been the biggest head-butting issue. We never had to answer to someone else about buying clothes or items for hobbies, for example, and we weren't about to start now," Tom says. Keeping a measure of financial independence helps them stay sane. "While we could shape our budget shares according to relative income, each of us would have to give up some independence over individual expenditures." Instead, Vilis paints houses to supplement his income, giving him the freedom to buy art (his hobby) without worrying Tom about their monthly budget.

FOUR WAYS TO SAVE

Here are four relatively painless tactics to help you and your honey set some money aside.

1. Set up (many) automatic deductions from your paycheck—to your 401(k), a government savings bond program, a brokerage account, or a savings account earmarked for one of your goals.

2. Start tracking your expenses—you'll probably end up curtailing them just to save yourself the bookkeeping trouble. Choose two or three categories

you think could use the most trimming (such as food or phone bills), and monitor those monthly.

3. Specifically budget "play money," and create an envelope with that money in cash. Give yourself permission to freely spend it—you'll feel rich! You'll likely spend less than if you had no budget. Remember, when the envelope is empty, you have to stay home.

4. Leave your credit card and checkbook at home when you go out. Make cash king. When you have to pull out actual dollar bills, you may find you're more reluctant to part with them.

For more money-saving tips, check out our online discussion board, Living Below Your Means, at boards.Fool.com.

My wife hadn't learned much about investing before we met. She thought it was a big gamble. After much discussion and a big leap of faith on her part, she opened those quarterly 401(k) statements and asks me what else we can do to put money away in the market. She now comes to *me* with new ideas on how to save! It's great.

—*David, married to Amy for six years*

Chapter 6

A Portfolio Built for Two

In this chapter, you and Hot Stuff will...

- Psych up to max out your savings.
- Set some long-term investing goals.
- Negotiate your investment risk.
- Learn the one investment strategy you need.

SHE LIKES STOCKS; HE LIKES BONDS. LET'S CALL THE WHOLE THING OFF.

Ah, investing! What could be more thrilling? More suspenseful? More exciting? To shamelessly steal from the old *Wide World of Sports* introduction: The thrill of victory! The agony of defeat! The hours of poring over 10-Q reports, balance sheets, and prospectuses!

Or maybe investing conjures the exact opposite reaction—hand-wringing, eye-rolling, sheer boredom, or outright fear—for you or your significant other.

Whether you're an investment junkie or a trepidatious novice, investing needs to be a part of your relationship. So what makes investing so complicated for couples? Gosh, where should we start? Let's see...

- One partner is more interested in the topic than the other.
- One partner is investing more money than the other.
- One or both partners don't like the delayed gratification investing requires.
- One partner is skipping work to day-trade your home equity loan.

Rest assured, there are ways to satisfy the risk-taker and worrywart in your relationship and set yourselves up for investing success. This is the perfect time in your *Couples & Cash* journey to bring up the topic of investing. You've had a few tough (but vital) conversations about money with your honey. You've gathered your important papers (bills, bank statements) and gotten all accounts in order. You have a solid list of goals, some of which probably require money to achieve. And after the last chapter, you probably have a better sense of where your cash is going and if you have any left to put away for the future.

So let's figure out how to make the most of that extra money and see how your and your honey's investing personalities mesh.

SETTING INVESTING GOALS

Setting investing goals may sound like a waste of time ("Hey, we just want to accumulate as much dough as we can! That's our goal!"), but no other topic is as important to your investing future. Don't skip this step.

When we talk about investing, we mean putting your *long-term savings* to work for you. At The Motley Fool, we define long term as five years, at the very least, and 10 years or longer, at best. We don't put money that we need to spend soon (tomorrow, next year, or even five years from now) into the stock market. So forget about trying to day-trade your way to the new flat-screen TV or genuine pleather couch. Not a good idea.

The market bounces around a lot in the short run and harshly punishes those forced to sell because they need invested money for immediate expenses. Don't be that guy.

Investing is for major expenses down the road. Perhaps you're investing for your child's future college tuition. Or maybe, just maybe, you'd actually like to retire when you're ready to stop working. (We've heard that some people are that way.) While it's certainly *possible* for investing to be fun and equally interesting for both partners, that doesn't necessarily mean it will be. That's OK. The important thing is that both of you agree on the *goal* of that investing.

The most crucial investing variable, by a landslide, is time. More specifically, the amount of time you can wait before you need the money. So be sure your goals have time frames. From a purely logical standpoint, the

FIVE CRITICAL QUESTIONS

When you consider your investment goals, ask the following questions and try to come to a consensus with your investing partner:

1. How much will we need to meet our goals?

2. How much time do we have? When are we most likely to need this invested money?

3. How serious would the consequences be if we cashed out on stocks early and lost a big chunk of this money?

4. How serious would the consequences be if we invested too conservatively and failed to meet our goals?

5. What type of investment vehicle (based on the level of potential return) offers us the best chance of meeting our goals with acceptable risk?

more time you have to meet your goal, the more risk you can take.

On the other hand, even time can't save you if your money is too conservatively invested. Paul and Rochelle, happily married with two adorable kids, wanted to know how long their retirement savings would last. (Though they joke about solving all their financial squabbles by having kids, thus eliminating all discretionary income.) Using their current retirement savings balance, they played around with a few assumptions—

HOW LONG WILL THE MONEY LAST?

If we earn this average annual return on retirement savings...	We'll run out of money when Rochelle (the younger partner) is:
6%	71
7%	75
8%	79
9%	85
10%	95
11%	$2.4 million remains when she hits 100
12%	$7.2 million remains when she hits 100

including how much they could contribute each year between now and retirement; how fast they are likely to spend money in retirement; what kind of return on investment they could earn safely during retirement; and average inflation of 3 percent.

Take a peek at the chart above to see what they discovered.

You and your honey can run the numbers on your retirement savings to see how long it will last, too. We have a host of calculators that let you consider various scenarios, just like Paul and Rochelle's. Click to www.Fool.com/retirement to check them out.

BECOME INVESTING PARTNERS

A good rule of thumb for investing partners is: Agree to agree. Yup, you read that right. When you're in it for the long haul, it's important to reach common ground for handling the family investments. Think of yourselves as co-CEOs of your financial empire.

Mark and Grace arrived at two primary long-term investment goals—retirement and college savings for their three bambinos—after a series of conversations. "Once we agreed on those, we put a plan in motion via automatic monthly investments," Mark explains. Autopilot provides the discipline for regular contributions and keeps the couple from agonizing over where to put each additional investment.

Mark, who is more interested in business and finance, generally evaluates these investments, and when he has a recommendation, he presents his case to Grace. Although the couple agrees on Mark's investment ideas most of the time, Grace often provides insights and asks questions that change the decisions. "There's no guaranteed rubber stamp at my house—thankfully," says Mark. "It's better described as a 'check-and-balance system'."

In a few rare instances, Mark has sold stock without telling Grace. "I felt terrible about it. Clearly my emotional desire to sell took over the rational," he says. He can attest to the fact that their conversations about money are much more pleasant when he runs his trading decisions by Grace before acting on them.

Just because Grace and Mark have an established investing game plan doesn't mean they no longer face challenges. Mark admits they are better long-term investors

than short-term money managers. And every life stage—
new jobs, more kids—presents a new financial picture.

Whatever your investment goals, discuss them, agree to
them, and commit them to paper. Writing things down,
as everybody knows, makes them more tangible and
easier to discuss. And you and your partner are going to
have plenty of discussions, particularly in the early
days of investing together.

RISKY BUSINESS

Now is a good time to discuss *how* you're going to invest.

Are you comfortable putting your money to work in the
stock market? What about your sweetie? Would s/he
rather put most of your dough in a money market account earning 3 percent interest? (If so, check out the
average return figures listed on page 73 under "Market
v. Mattress".)

What if investing partners have substantially different investing styles and levels of risk tolerance? That's an excellent question. Before you can reap the deep and lasting
benefits of investing as a couple, you really have to settle
on what level of risk you can tolerate *as a couple.* This may
mean being less aggressive than the more investment-
savvy partner might like. It might also mean being more
aggressive than the more risk-averse partner might like.

Whoever said a perfect compromise is when no one
walks away completely happy was right. When you

decide to invest as a couple, you're giving up your my-way-or-the-highway rights, which is precisely the way it should be. No one said this was going to be easy.

But it will be rewarding. Remember the ground rules we established in Chapter 2? Now's a good time to add a few investing ground rules. These can be as concise or expansive as you require, but they should at least include an agreed-upon dollar amount for the investment account and an assessment of each partner's risk level.

Consider the investing ground rules reached by Shannon, a self-admitted investing geek, and his risk-averse bride, Kristin:

- Their first-choice investment each year is maxing out their 401(k)s and IRAs by contributing the most allowed by Uncle Sam.

- Any leftovers default to an index tracker, except...

- When Shannon can make a compelling case for investing in an individual company, Kristin is open to persuasion (especially when Ben Kweller tickets are presented with the investment overview).

That last point has been crucial for Shannon. As the more enthusiastic investor, it's important to him to know that when he feels strongly about a company (meaning he believes it can earn more than the S&P's annual average), Kristin can be convinced. For the record, this has happened exactly five times over 14 years of investing as a couple.

The How Low Is Too Low? exercise on page 120 will help you and your honey assess how much risk you can handle. Take a moment to answer the three questions posed and discuss your answers as a couple.

THE ONLY INVESTMENT YOU MAY EVER NEED

Investing partners should also agree to a definition of investment success. Try something simple, such as "keeping pace with a broader market index." That's an excellent place to start, and for millions of intelligent investors, an excellent place to finish, too. There are a number of easy ways to achieve this important goal.

For a very long time, the stock market has been the place to be for nearly all long-term investors. There are a variety of ways to put your money to work for you in the market. Heck, practically the entire Motley Fool is devoted to talking about saving and investing strategies.

But you don't need to spend years honing your stock-picking skills to keep pace with the market. In fact, one of the simplest ways to put your money to work for you is to invest in a special mutual fund called an index fund.

The S&P 500 Index Fund (the Standard and Poor's 500 Index, which tracks the performance of 500 of the leading and most profitable U.S. companies) has risen 13.6 percent annually over the last 50 years, on average. That means if you invested $10,000 into the S&P 500 50 years ago, today you'd be able to call your discount broker, sell your position for $5.78 million, patriotically pay down your taxes of $1.62 million, and end up with $4.16 million.

Quite a feat, yes?

What's more astonishing is that the plain, old, unsexy index fund has provided investors with better returns than more than 80 percent of actively managed mutual funds. Why? You're paying extra for an actively managed fund, and not because some wizard behind the curtain is running a tab by trading in and out of stocks all day. Extra fees for taxes, marketing expenses, and a well-paid fund manager prevent the majority of actively managed mutual funds from keeping pace with the market's average returns. Ouch! That's some bill.

If you're looking for the easiest way to get average investment returns (and that means besting more than 80 percent of Wall Streeters), we think index funds are just peachy.

KEEPING TRACK

Once you've made the decision to invest, saving will obviously take on new importance. Long-term investing, in fact, is really long-term *saving*. Financial tracking software, such as Quicken or Microsoft Money, can help organize your finances. And believe us, nothing inspires saving like seeing your own finances and spending habits displayed as pie charts. Yikes.

MARKET V. MATTRESS

People are wary of "the market" for many valid reasons. Perhaps they're scared of investing because it seems so complicated. For some, the market feels too risky of a place for their money. But being too conservative with your money can end up being riskier than too aggressive. Take a gander at these figures:

- Had you put $1 into Treasury bills (or more recently, a money market account) in 1900, you would have about $40 today.

- Had you put $1 into bonds in 1900, you would have about $42 today.

- Had you put $1 into stocks in 1900, you would have more than $10,000 today.

- Had you put a buck into your lousy checking account, you'd owe something like $4,000 in ATM fees. (OK, we made that last number up, but you get the point.)

The most important part of investing as a couple is keeping your partner in the loop. Investment partners should agree on a regular schedule for financial discussions. Quarterly reports seem to have caught on in the business world and will probably work just fine for couples who invest Foolishly, too. The level of detail these reports require is up to you and your partner, of course, but at the very least, include the following information:

- The amount currently invested.
- The percent change from the previous quarter.

- Any transactions (most typically buying, selling, and brokerage fees) that have occurred since the previous quarter.

Investing will be a life-long pursuit. Take some time now, as a couple, to set yourselves up for a long and illustrious investment partnership.

8 RULES OF INVESTING WITH YOUR SPOUSE

Here are some tips for twosomes from Barbara, a long-time wife, Fool, and investor:

1. **Communicate.** Share your feelings, experiences, hopes, and dreams—both positive and negative.

2. **Initiate.** Become the leader in developing a healthy investing plan for your family. Don't count on your partner to bring up the subject, or you may never begin.

3. **Educate.** Be a sponge and keep absorbing. Share as much knowledge as your spouse is willing to hear. Fess up to errors, explaining what you learned from them. To err is to be human; forgive each other for inevitable missed investing opportunities, such as buying too late or selling too soon.

4. **Invigorate.** The more fun you can make investing, the more receptive your partner will be. Sharing your vision of a brighter future will make a brighter future, and your excitement will be contagious.

5. **Deliberate.** Think about and discuss issues and decisions carefully. You're not always going to agree, so determine what is and isn't important. If a disagreement is irreconcilable, consider establishing separate brokerage accounts. This way, different investing styles can flourish, and there's no room for recrimination—only merciless teasing.

6. **Negotiate.** Sometimes you have to give a little. Spend time trying to arrive at decisions that serve you both. If both partners have "us" as the first priority, everything is negotiable.

7. **Cooperate.** Marital bliss doesn't occur during a constant tug-of-war; a hug-of-war is better. No matter what causes your resistance to the investing process, give it your all and be your family's chief co-operating officer.

8. **Celebrate.** Make all wins special events. If your spouse is resistant to investing but inches toward cooperation by picking up a business journal, acknowledge and celebrate the progress. Don't neglect small movements from your partner, even if it's merely a willingness to remain open to discussion.

All families need to have some difficult conversations. While it's no fun to think about death or incapacity, the possibility is inevitable. By putting in place just a few important documents, things for my wife and daughters will be far easier—and quite possibly far cheaper—should something happen to either of us. All it took was a bit of discussion and a visit to a qualified attorney. The cost is minimal compared to the peace of mind we have.

—*David, married to Betty Jo for 42 years*

Chapter 7

What Your Honey *Has* to Know

When you two starry-eyed kids are done with this chapter, you will...

- Probably need a new box of Kleenex.
- Know how to protect your loved ones from financial hardship.
- Be inspired to share your safety net.
- Have a checklist of your life's labors.

ACCIDENTS HAPPEN

We've come into some irrefutable information: According to most physicians, there's a 100 percent chance you will die. While we're on this grim topic, you should also know that 10 out of 10 insurance agents claim there's a one-in-three chance you will be disabled for three months or more before age 50. They further claim that for most folks, there's a far greater chance of disability than death prior to that age.

What do these frightening certainties mean for you and your honey? Barring Armageddon or the total collapse of society (we're willing to concede that these require no financial plan), life will go on after you. And some sad soul—likely one of your favorite people—will be stuck wrapping up your affairs. To make it worse, along the road to this certain end point, there's a good chance you'll be at least temporarily incapable of managing your financial affairs. (We're relentless, aren't we?)

Just for a few moments, consider the possibility that something—a bad something—happens to you. Will the important people in your life know what to do? Will they be prepared to do it? And just what do they need to know, anyway?

Wait! There's good news.

It doesn't take much to put a few safeguards in place so you don't have to worry about this stuff, and you can get on, skipping through life, with that smile we love so much.

Here's all you have to do:
1. Complete four important documents.
2. Make your heirs apparent.
3. Let important people know where your stuff is.

See? That budgeting chapter wasn't so bad after all, compared to this! But you know what they say: When life gives you lemons, lawyers will find a way to get 40 percent of all lemonade proceeds. Here's more information on these sunny issues.

LIFE GOES ON

Your loved ones need to know a lot about your personal finances, assets, desires, and where you keep the dog's heartworm pills. In fact, they need to know as much about those things as you do.

It makes no difference whether you're married or not. You must determine how your loved ones can and will act for you when you can no longer act for yourself. This is particularly true for unmarried couples. Often, unless the necessary legal documents are in place, family members of the incapacitated or deceased person will throw sand in the gears by deliberately excluding or ignoring that person's life partner. Therefore, it behooves all couples to do some contingency planning to make sure things happen as they desire.

AVOIDING HASSLES FOR UNMARRIEDS

Unmarried couples face a myriad of legal issues when it comes to estate planning and medical directives. Still, many institutions will give opposite-sex couples a break because it's a much more familiar arrangement.

Same-sex couples need to be extra careful to plan legally because some institutions are unfamiliar with, and sometimes even hostile toward, their relationships. Consider how Tom and his partner, Vilis, tackled these important issues. "We realized we needed to lock in our rights as a couple with clear legal arrangements," says Tom. Many institutions, such as hospitals, won't allow same-sex couples to make medical decisions without pieces of paper in front of them.

"We actually took about two years and a year of living together to begin planning," he says. The first step in tackling these important issues came as it does for many unmarried couples—buying a house together. "After determining that we both had our finances in order, we made sure we owned the house through joint tenancy, with the right of survivorship." (You don't want joint tenancy with right of survivorship if one of you is a financial loser because the whole kit and caboodle can be grabbed to cover the debt.)

Next, they moved onto wills and durable powers of attorney. They used a low-cost, pre-paid legal service provided through Tom's employer. "Contractual legal arrangements for unmarried couples of all types (from marital attachments to business partnerships) are common, so the attorney asked all the right questions and handled it routinely," he says. The couple made one another executors and named friends and family as backups. "While they know our preferences for things that don't go in wills (such as cremation), we really wanted to put everything in writing to offer some guidance. In the event of a tragic double death, for example, having our wishes in writing would help others implement them, especially when under pressure."

TOP FIVE WAYS TO MAKE YOUR LOVED ONES MISERABLE

1. Execute a durable power of attorney naming your daughter to speak for you when you can't, but forget to make her signatory on the safe-deposit box where you store the document.

2. Take out a long-term disability policy, but neglect to tell your spouse. Then go into a coma for six months so that Snookums has to take out a second mortgage to pay the bills.

3. Play a good joke on the poor soul who will complete your final tax form, and leave your important papers under mountains of less important papers scattered all over the house.

4. Get divorced and forget to change the beneficiary on your life insurance policy. That way, your first husband—the lunatic who ran off with the Krishnas—gets the lump-sum death benefit, while your second husband and family of 50 years get zip.

5. Forget to tell your wife about that great new financial planner you're working with—the one who mysteriously boards a flight for the Cayman Islands the day of your unexpected demise.

Grim? Yes. Necessary? Absolutely.

THE ESSENTIAL DOCUMENTS
Clearly it helps to have all of this information in one place, just in case the unthinkable happens. Although

it's not the most exciting way to spend an evening, a little time spent organizing your important papers and creating or updating your will can save your family and friends *a lot* of trouble down the road.

We've taken the liberty of making your job a little easier. (Yay!) On pages 121–128, we provide a handy checklist to help in your contingency preparations. Go over it with your partner. Then make sure both of you know how the items in that list apply, in case something happens to your better half. It will solve a number of problems for both of you, if necessary.

Here are the most important documents:

Your Will (Last Will and Testament)
What is it: Your will details exactly what happens to your property (and potentially your minor dependents) when you die.

Where to get it: We recommend you see an attorney. It won't cost you much, and you'll get it done quickly and correctly. If you opt for preprinted, fill-in-the-blanks forms and software, be sure they are updated and conform to the laws of your state.

Living Will (Advance Medical Directive)
What is it: This says you want the right to die a natural death, free of all costly, extraordinary efforts to keep you alive, when your life can only be sustained by artificial means.

Where to get it: This document is available free at virtually every hospital in the nation.

Durable Power of Attorney *and* Medical Power of Attorney (Healthcare Proxy)

What is it: These documents allow the person you select to make decisions on your behalf (financial and legal, in the first case; medical, in the second case) when you are incapacitated.

Where to get it: We suggest you see an attorney for these, too.

HEALTH AND MEDICAL CARE

Your loved ones should know your wishes for health and medical care. Discuss the use of life-support systems when there is no reasonable expectation of recovery and your wishes for organ donation. Remember, prior to age 50, it's far more likely to be mentally or physically incapacitated than to die. Obtaining the legal documents we've listed will permit your loved ones to act on your behalf without a court order, saving thousands in attorney expenses, court fees, and a lot of time—far more than the small cost of drafting these documents now.

FUNERAL ARRANGEMENTS

Your loved ones should also know your funeral arrangement desires—whether you want the "Fairway to Heaven" casket or the "Elvis (The Thin Years)" urn. Knowing your wishes in advance will ensure relatives aren't pressured into high-cost services because they're making decisions during a time of grief.

LAST WILL AND TESTAMENT AND/OR LIVING OR TESTAMENTARY TRUSTS

Review these documents to make sure they clearly express your wishes and intent. If you have personal property not included in these documents, specify through an addendum or codicil how these personal effects are to be distributed. If these documents have not been developed yet, or if a lawyer hasn't reviewed them in more than five years, get thee to an attorney! If you have minor children, specify who their guardian should be in the event both parents are deceased.

Be aware that a failure to execute this document prior to your death will almost certainly cause your family to struggle through your state's probate process. In addition, the state will almost certainly dictate a distribution of your assets that does not match your desires. So please, don't put this off.

NAMING BENEFICIARIES

Not everything will pass to your loved ones via your will. Some assets (such as real estate, residences, taxable investment accounts, and checking accounts) may be owned as joint tenancy property. If that's the case, when you die, they will pass outside of your will to the joint owner. Additionally, things like retirement accounts and life insurance policies require a designated beneficiary or two. Those proceeds will go to the designated persons upon the owner's death, which means your will won't govern the distribution of these assets.

The moral here is that, in addition to completing your will, you should *consider two things:*

1. Ownership of your home, bank accounts, taxable brokerage accounts: Are they jointly or individually titled/owned?
2. Beneficiaries on all retirement accounts (including 401(k), 403(b), pension, profit sharing, and IRAs) and insurance policies: Keep 'em up to date!

Review this information whenever a major life event occurs (marriage, divorce, birth, death, a really bad haircut). You can get the necessary forms to change beneficiaries from your human resources department (for employer-provided insurance and retirement plans) or from the insurance company, brokerage, mutual fund, or IRA provider for personal insurance policies and investment/retirement accounts.

AVOIDABLE TRAGEDIES

Long time Fool, David, and his wife, Betty Jo, have been married for more than half of their lives. Heed David's advice:

"During that time, we have watched friends and family struggle with what to do when the unforeseen happens. We've seen the impact on families when someone is in a coma and unable to make medical decisions or manage assets. We know the problems that arise when

FOR RICHER OR POORER... AGAIN

First comes love, then comes marriage. Then comes divorce and the blush of a new love, marriage again, and the host of financial issues that plague most couples the first and second (and eighth and ninth) time around.

Consumer Reports offers some financial guidance for couples who remarry. The report gives the following advice for a smooth financial transition:

- Disclose your finances to each other. (Yes, even that five-figure amount you owe to Mr. MasterCard.)

- Complete a prenuptial or postnuptial agreement to identify the assets each of you is bringing to the marriage. It should also spell out who gets what, should your starry-eyed love flicker out or if one partner— gulp—dies.

- Set up a new family budget and determine how you'll pay joint expenses.

- Decide how to title your joint assets. After all, you don't want your ex laying claim to your stuff.

- Develop a new estate plan, including new wills, durable powers of attorney, living wills, healthcare proxies, and trusts.

- Adjust the dependency exemption on your tax withholding, and review your insurance policies to make sure you have the proper life and disability coverage for additional dependents.

someone dies without a will. We know too well the pain survivors feel when insurance policy beneficiaries were not changed after a marriage, divorce, and/or birth."

How do you comfort the spouse who needs cash but is unable to tap into an investment account because he isn't a joint owner? How do you ease the pain of someone whose partner would certainly not have consented to further medical treatment, yet that treatment continues, at great cost, because the family doesn't have the legal authority to cease it? What do you say to someone who learns her loved one's life insurance will go to an old flame because the deceased forgot to change the policy when he got married?

"Believe us when we say adequate answers to any of these questions are hard to find," David says. But those questions don't have to be answered for those who take the appropriate actions.

GETTING ORGANIZED

It doesn't do any good to have your affairs in order, all of your important papers filed, and your beneficiaries up to date if no one knows where to find your records.

Well, today's your lucky day because we just happen to provide—at no additional cost to you—a handy-dandy Really Important Stuff Checklist on pages 121–128. It's mind-numbingly comprehensive, so take it one bite at a time. But it's important, so spend a few minutes per week filling it out until you're done.

We'll leave you with two final thoughts that will exhibit your enduring love. (OK, that may be a bit overstated, but just play along.)

1. When you're done filling out the checklist, make copies of the completed sheet and leave them in two safe places. The person to whom you assign durable power of attorney should know exactly where to find a copy. Note: If this person is not a signatory on your safe-deposit box, s/he won't be able to get into the box.

2. Tell your family where you keep the list! Make a few copies and give them to trusted friends and relatives. There's only one thing worse than filling out a dead guy's tax forms, and that's doing it without access to his financial records. Believe us— your posse will thank you posthumously.

3. Note where your loved ones can find available liquid cash to meet immediate needs. During times of distress and grief, little thought may be given to this detail. List all available sources your partner may use, such as checking, savings, and investment accounts.

Everything gets easier the more a marriage matures. Of course, this doesn't happen automatically; it takes the most earnest kind of soul work. A marriage is only as mature as the people in it. It takes letting go of trying to change another person, winking at flaws, affirming the best, having a generous heart, constantly learning, and keeping a sense of humor. If you work at it, how could you *not* get better at handling everything— money included?

—Joan, married to George for 40 years

Practice Makes Perfect

By the time you two kids have reached the last page, you will have...
- Scheduled a quarterly economic summit.
- Tackled the most essential personal finance topics.
- Basked in the afterglow of your first-ever financial summit.

THE PARTY'S ONLY JUST BEGUN

We're like: "Here we are, at the final chapter of *The Motley Fool's Guide to Couples & Cash* already!"

And you're *totally* like: "Too soon! Snookums hasn't saved a single latte receipt yet! [Long pause.] OK, the truth is that we're both still looking for the checkbook. Are we doomed?"

And we're *so* like: "Of course not. Just getting this far in the book puts you, like, *way* ahead of the average couple."

And we mean it. Even if you've just skimmed the book, chances are you've soaked up some knowledge. And all the resources are still at your disposal. Now it's just a matter of making the time to use them. That's the goal of this final chapter—to provide a concrete, bare-minimum game plan for carving out this time together.

YOUR ECONOMIC SUMMIT

The next time you get up to get a glass of water, turn out your reading light, or discipline an unruly child, grab your calendar. Now, while the iron is hot, resolve to spend 90 minutes once every three months discussing your finances. This four-time yearly urge to meet will become as strong as flowers in the spring and pumpkins at the end of October. Make it a special occasion. Serve refreshments. Reward yourselves afterward. Get a babysitter. Put out a press release. Just do whatever it takes.

During this financial summit with your spouse, you'll cover the two most essential topics in all of personal finance—emergency planning and getting your money to work for you.

Sound simple? Feel motivated? If you took even a halfway heroic stab at it in Chapter 3, you already have most of the necessary data in hand. All you need to do is follow our proposed summit agenda.

PREPARE FOR THE MEETING

It's time for pre-game! Let's get ourselves in a position

JUST FOUR TIMES A YEAR

Hey, this isn't like signing up for aerobics! We're only talking about *90 minutes, four times a year* to hold a financial summit with your best pal. If you just practice this regular habit of focused communication, you will learn to:

- Communicate productively about money on a regular basis, with a simple, structured agenda to get you started.

- Sleep better, worry less, and bring less underlying emotional baggage to the relationship by knowing that your emergency financial needs are covered.

- Focus on the big-picture financial plan, where—free of the often-volatile details—there is the greatest likelihood of consensus and a shared vision.

to win this one. Go through the handy Meeting Prep Checklist on page 129, and sign yourselves up for half each. Most of the financial records should be handy, since you went through them earlier in the book (throat clearing).

THE SUMMIT AGENDA

We'll give a brief overview of your summit agenda here. Everything you need for your summit—including leading questions that'll get your finances in tiptop shape—is detailed starting on page 130. There you'll find helpful charts and a few additional tips. We've tried to take all the guesswork out of it. Aren't we thoughtful?

PRIORITY ONE: PREPARING FOR FINANCIAL EMERGENCIES

Odds are good that one of you values security and peace of mind more than anything else money can buy. If this describes your partner, resolve to provide these things for him/her in good measure. Be a big kid. Don't quibble over the details.

1. **Review disability, life, and health insurance plans.**

Ideally, these insurance questions are reviewed at every family "life event" (a birth, marriage, job change, death), but this quick quarterly review will serve as an important backup plan.

In particular, pay attention to often-overlooked disability insurance. The effects of permanent disability can be just as devastating to your dependents' financial security as your death.

Next consider your life insurance. It's possible to insure anybody's life, whether they're working or not, but Fools typically buy it only to cover wage earners and caregivers with dependents. The question to ask is: "What would happen to my dependents, financially, should they lose my income." If the answer is pretty ugly, then you might want to get your life insured, ASAP.

Health insurance is too complex a topic for a quick review summit, but we've included a few key questions in your agenda.

2. Monitor the growth of your family emergency fund.

The goal here is liquid savings (*not* stocks or tax-sheltered retirement plans) equal to at least three to six months of regular household expenses. Many couples can testify that the tenor of their personal finance world made a big U-turn on the day they established this cushion. Even if debt limits your ability to save, make at least token $100 quarterly contributions to this fund.

Try your darndest to leave this savings cushion untapped. We can think of six good reasons to make this a priority:

1. It provides a buffer between your living expenses and your retirement savings, which gives you some time to adjust to an emergency—such as losing your job—before the situation erodes your savings.

2. Though an ideal budget should account for some savings toward maintenance and replacement of things like major appliances, an emergency fund can be your backup when it comes to these unexpected budget busters.

3. Building an emergency stash will show you, viscerally—away from the bright lights and giant swings of the stock market—how much discipline it takes to save. Any pain that results will help motivate you to keep your hands off the fund and to stay out of debt.

4. You'll learn the joy of regularly *receiving* interest payments. No matter how bad a day you're having, you can smile knowing that some money is working for you.

5. You'll sleep better knowing it's there.

PRIORITY TWO: MAKE MORE MONEY THAN YOU SPEND

The second agenda topic is about easing your financial wagon toward the high road, gently but firmly. Ultimately, it all comes down to making more money than you spend on a regular basis. Get ahead and let your money work while you sleep, work, and walk hand in hand, barefoot, through the grass. Heck, it even works while you fight with each other or zone out in front of the tube watching *Trading Spaces.*

Get behind, though, and not only are you battling this cruel ol' world on a daily basis, but you're adding to somebody else's bank account (Mr. Visa, perhaps?) as you go.

So, if you get nothing else out of this book, look at one another right now and repeat after us: "We are committed, as a couple, to making more money than we spend on a regular basis. We won't rest until we get there, and once we get there, we'll stay there." Then add: "Aren't those Motley Fools cool?"

Here's how to stick with that pledge:

1. Review your total debt load.

Add up all consumer debt, including credit cards and automobile loans. In most cases, you'll want to include student loans, unless after-tax savings' interest payments are below 8 percent and/or these loans offer important flexibility in payment schedule. Don't include your mortgage. Paying down this low-interest, tax-sheltered loan is a thorny issue, and not necessarily a good idea, so mortgage loans fall outside the scope of this simple debt review. Turn to the chart on page 135 to track your progress. Simply record the total amount owed and interest rate paid, by debt.

2. Tally contributions to your retirement savings.

Unless you like the prospect of powerless old age, no savings goal is more important than a decent retirement. The kids may or may not get into Harvard, and the family car may or may not make it through the next year, but odds are excellent that you'll want—or need—to retire. See how you're doing by filling out the Retirement Savings Worksheet on page 138.

3. Plan an additional savings goal.

In addition to your emergency fund and retirement, it helps to have at least one additional savings goal. If debt is your No. 1 problem, this may have to wait, but reaffirming this shared vision will boost your joint motivation to pay down the debt. If you're not in a position to save much toward these goals at the moment, their existence will help to motivate you during moments of fiscal weakness.

4. Set the next date for your summit.

At a minimum, make a date to spend 90 minutes together once every three months, or as the business guys like to say, *quarterly*.

LOVE, AND MONEY, GO ON

Chip and Jeanne have been married for more than 30 years. Consider how their lives—in a financial context—have changed:

In the beginning:
- No money
- No children, and soon after, young children
- New job
- New house
- $58,000 of mortgage debt
- $10,000 in life insurance
- No retirement savings

Today:

- Some money
- Three grown children
- Established job
- Bigger house
- $205,000 of mortgage debt
- $650,000 in life insurance
- $420,000 in retirement savings

"Our finances have gotten easier as our earnings have increased," Chip observes. "The stress was much higher when facing the future costs of educating three children than it seems today, when facing retirement in the next 15 years." Still, the complexity of the couple's assets has grown exponentially over the course of their marriage. And money issues continue to get more complex as the couple helps their grown children get established ("and learn to do their own tax returns").

But even after 30 years of marriage, some things never change: "The recurring money issue in our relationship has been that I usually get grouchy when I pay bills—always have. Jeanne avoids me and goes to bed early, leaving me to get grouchy alone."

Beyond that, this couple keeps money issues in perspective. "Our primary satisfaction has never come from money," Jeanne says. "We never fought that much about money because we remain happy with what we have—and happy to live on whatever we make."

Family, faith, a biannual road trip, and rousing games of charades around the dinner table are the core of this couple's happiness. Money just enables them to spoil the kids rotten during Christmas and enjoy an occasional good scotch. Isn't love a beautiful thing?

FOUR TIPS FOR A LIFETIME OF FINANCIAL BLISS

Human nature and busy lives have a knack for putting off life's little inconveniences—like dealing with your finances. Simply reading this *Couples & Cash Guide* (or flipping through, as you might be doing right now in Aisle 17: Relationship Management/Hot Rod Racing Paperbacks), you've already cleared the first hurdle. You've acknowledged that this is an area worth improving. Your heart is in the right place. Aww, you big lug.

Now it's time to keep the momentum going.

1. Make a resolution to make money a nonissue in your relationship. Consider it simply the means to making your joint dreams come true. It's all about perspective.

2. Schedule regular money discussions with your honey. At the very least, use your quarterly economic summit to fall back on. Let this meeting serve as the North Star of your joint financial journey. Doing so will bolster your couplehood, both financially and—perhaps more important to your life together—emotionally.

3. Make communication and understanding the de facto mode for your money talks. When it comes to tackling the stickier issues of life as a couple—like whose turn it is to pay the bills—these skills are essential. With them, nothing can crack the force field of your burning passion for one another.

4. Lastly, congratulate yourselves. Seriously, take a moment right now and do just that. And every time you successfully wend your way through a joint financial decision, remember to pat yourselves on the back.

Congratulations! You've laid the base for better results in the years to come, through regular communication and joint planning. We thank you from the bottom of our Foolish hearts for letting us play a small role in helping you and your honey better handle money together.

Couples & Cash Worksheets

CHAPTER 1: HE SPENDS, SHE SPENDS
Lights! Action! Welcome to The Fooly-Wed Game!

Take a few minutes to answer the following questions. Don't peek at one another's answers. The fun part of this exercise is comparing your responses at the end.

1. Who is responsible for balancing the checkbook?

   _____

2. Who is the long-term planner?

   _____

3. When was the last time you made financial whoopee? Or at least *talked* about your finances?

   _____

4. On a scale of 1-5 (1 is "not very," and 5 is "very"), how important is it that you and your partner:
   - Cut coupons _____
   - Go to the gas station with the cheapest gas _____
   - Rent videos instead of going to movies _____
   - Comparison shop? _____

5. How much is too much to spend:
   - On going out to dinner? $____
   - Without talking to your partner first? $____
   - On gifts (for each other, for children, for relatives and friends)? $____
   - On vacation? $____

6. If your spouse's money personality were a super-hero, which superhero would it be?

   _____

7. If you inherited $10,000, it would be most important to: 1) pay off debt; 2) buy a new car; 3) invest the money; 4) take a vacation; 5) throw an awesome party for the rest of your relatives so that they, too, can see what a great niece, grand-daughter, and 19th cousin you are?

   _____

8. When do you expect to buy your next car? Will it be used or new? What kind?

   _____

   _____

9. What are your top three long-term financial goals?

   _____

   _____

   _____

10. Harry Potter *v.* Spiderman? Discuss.

    _____

Results!

Great! Now it's time to take your financial temperature. As you compare answers, note where you agreed and disagreed ("hot topics," if you will). As you proceed through this guide, you and your partner can refer back to your personal list of hot topics and tackle these areas of tension when you are ready.

- Able to get through the first five questions without an argument? Congratulations! You two could put the "gold" in golden years. Call the neighbor's kids and tell those whippersnappers the secret to your great relationship.

- Laughed some, cried some, yelled a little bit? You're communicating, all right! Chapter 2 can help you and your partner to find less volatile ways to get fiscally fit.

- Was your financial whoopee less satisfying than you'd hoped? Don't give up. Throughout this guide, other couples shared their experiences and encouragement. So stick with it.

CHAPTER 2: GETTING IN THE MOOD (FOR A MONEY TALK)

Use this Big Talk Prep Worksheet to put on paper your commitment to a productive and fun money conversation.

1. **Set a date.** Pick out the setting for your money talk.

2. **Prepare for the post-game fallout.** Make an Emergency Relationship Repair Kit. Take a toolbox (or any old box) and place inside items that will help you get over a spat with your spouse.

3. **Set your ground rules.** Feel free to borrow the ground rules listed in the chapter, or write your own.

4. **Prepare to scrimmage.** Turn to Chapter 3 to start The Big Game.

The Big Talk Prep Worksheet

Date: ___ / ___ / ___

Setting: _____

Refreshments: _____

Reward:_____

Emergency Relationship Repair Kit Contents:

_____

_____

_____

_____

_____

_____

_____

_____

_____

Our Ground Rules:

As a first step toward compromise, alternate who gets to propose each rule.

1. _____
_____
_____

2. _____
_____
_____

3. _____
_____
_____

4. _____
_____
_____

5. _____
_____
_____

Extra Notes:

_____
_____
_____
_____
_____
_____

CHAPTER 3: THE STATE OF THE UNION
Net Worth Worksheet
Let's start tallying. On page 110 is a brief Net Worth Worksheet. We've included "his and hers" columns, if you're interested in tracking your net worth that way (some unmarried couples or those with previous marriages may choose to go this route). But you can only use those two columns if you promise to be nice about it.

Optional
Compiling a truly comprehensive list of where your money is (your balance sheet) can take time. So even after a few weeks, if you and your beloved only had time to add up the dollar amounts of some of your basic accounts, that's great. Really, we mean it! By doing even the *simplest* overview of your assets and liabilities, you've gotten a better sense of where you stand financially than, well, most people.

Net Worth Cheat Sheet
Want a ballpark estimate of where you and your sweetheart stand financially? Here are a few leading questions that'll give you a pretty good picture. If you have a sense of some of these figures, it shouldn't take you more than six minutes and 34 seconds to fill out.

- Guesstimate how much you have in various bank accounts (checking, savings, money market).

- Give a ballpark figure for how much you have in brokerage and retirement accounts (this includes stocks, bonds, mutual funds, IRAs, and 401(k)s).

  _____

- What's an approximate figure for the worth of your home, cars, and any other valuable items.

  _____

- Now add 'em up. These are your assets.

  _____

- How much do you owe (mortgage, car loans, credit cards, and any other miscellaneous debt)? Don't pull out the calculator—just estimate. These are your liabilities. _____

- OK, now take the number you got for your assets and subtract your liabilities. Whatever's left over is your (approximate) net worth.

  _____

NET WORTH WORKSHEET

	Ours	His	Hers
ASSETS			
Cash:			
Checking accounts			
Savings accounts/CDs			
Cash in brokerage accounts			
Money market accounts			
Long-Term Savings/Investments:			
IRAs			
401(k)s			
Stocks, bonds, mutual funds			
Other investments			
Exercised stock options			
Cash value of life insurance			
Fixed Assets:			
Housing			
Jewelry (optional)			
Cars (optional)			
Total Assets			
LIABILITIES			
Short-Term Debt:			
Credit cards			
Bank loans and lines of credit			
Store charge accounts			
Long-Term Debt:			
Mortgage			
Home-equity loans			
Student loans			
Car loans			
Total Liabilities			
Total Assets – Total Liabilities = NET WORTH			

CHAPTER 4: SETTING PRIORITIES

Together, jot down all the goals that come to mind:

1. _____
2. _____
3. _____
4. _____
5. _____
6. _____
7. _____
8. _____
9. _____
10. _____

Now whittle those down by answering the following questions:

Q: Do you have debts to pay off? _____

Q: Are the necessities taken care of? _____

Q: What major life events are you expecting in the next three to five years?

_____

_____

_____

The answers should give you a little more perspective on how your "wish list" matches up with reality. Now have each partner write down his/her Top 5 list separately, and then compare notes.

TOP 5 WISH LIST

Partner 1:	Partner 2:
1. _____	1. _____
2. _____	2. _____
3. _____	3. _____
4. _____	4. _____
5. _____	5. _____

Take a look at where you agree and talk through any disagreements. Now compile a new list of joint goals.

1. _____
2. _____
3. _____
4. _____
5. _____

What's It Gonna Cost?

How are you going to pay for these dreams?

Systematically, that's how. Figure out how much you need to save to achieve each goal, then break that amount into monthly (or even per-paycheck) figures—and be sure to factor in any cash you've already saved toward each goal. Maybe you need to save $100 a month toward a vacation, $300 toward a house, and $200 toward retirement.

Use this chart to keep track of how much you need to save toward each goal:

SAVINGS GOALS

Goal	Date to Achieve It By	Total Cost	Cost per Month (or per paycheck)
Goal 1			
Goal 2			
Goal 3			
Goal 4			
Goal 5			

CHAPTER 5: ...AND BUDGET MAKES THREE

There are many ways to devise a budget. Here we present three: the Baby Budget, the Half-Baked Budget, and the Whole-Baked Budget.

If you choose to do the Whole-Baked Budget, start by reviewing your statements for the past four months, then calculate a monthly average and fill in the worksheet on pages 118–119.

Half-Baked Budgeters: Review your statements for the past month (or week, or—for the truly under-cooked—three days) and fill in the categories on page 117. High fives all around!

If neither of the Baked Budgets is to your liking, we draw your attention to the Baby Budget's top-down approach. Essentially, the formula is: Income – Fixed Expenses *(including savings)* = Discretionary Money

Remember to first list the goals you created in Chapter 4. This is the real purpose of a budget: *to make sure you achieve your goals.* Next fill in the actual amount and analyze the data. Then consider the following:

- Are you sufficiently funding your goals?

- Is there a considerable amount of money going to stuff that doesn't add much to your quality of life?

- Calculate how much more you'd have if you could cut 5 percent from your variable expenses (food, clothing, entertainment).

Discuss the categories with each other and fill in the budget amount for each item.

The Baby Budget
Ready? Set? Budget!

First, gather one month's worth of paychecks. Congratulations! You've just finished the *income* side of the ledger.

On the *expenses* side, aim not to track every penny, but to see how many discretionary pennies are actually available. Start with just the basic, unavoidable monthly costs—the easy stuff to estimate:

- Total housing costs (rent, mortgage payment)

- Grocery costs (assume you never eat out)

- Utilities (average your highest and lowest bills from the past year for electricity, gas, heating oil, water, phone)

- Transportation costs (gas, bus fare)

- Annual insurance bills divided by 12

- Loan payments

- Credit card minimums

Now, add up all these must-do monthly bills and subtract the total from your monthly income. The equation should look something like this:

Monthly Income – Must-Do Monthly Bills = $ _____

This difference represents your monthly discretionary income. If you're like most people, this slice of the cake ain't what you thought it would be. This is especially true when you take the next step, *perhaps the most important budgeting step of all:* Add some savings to the non-discretionary, must-pay pile.

Just getting this far in the budget process could turn your ship around. Exactly how much savings to add and exactly how to split up the discretionary income are still important. But this is usually where the work and arguments start, so make sure you put the cart in front of the horse before you set off for the longer ride—especially if you're not sure you'll ever get to it.

If you want to dig a little deeper and review more categories, try the Half-Baked Budget on page 117.

For the overachievers and the truly committed, try your hand at the Whole-Baked Budget presented on pages 118–119.

HALF-BAKED BUDGET

Half-Baked Budget period ended ___ / ___ / ___
Goals We're Trying to Achieve:

	Actual	Budget	First Review
Income:	$	$	$
Salary/wages/commissions/bonus			
Interest/dividends			
Other income			
Total Income	$	$	$
Expenses:	$	$	$
Savings			
Goal #1			
Goal #2			
Goal #3			
Rent/mortgage			
Utilities			
Maintenance			
Automobile			
Clothing			
Medical/dental care			
Entertainment			
Food			
Child-related expenses			
Vacations			
Gifts and charity			
Insurance			
Loan payments			
Miscellaneous out-of-pocket expenses			
Other (list):			
Total Expenses	$	$	$
CASH SURPLUS (DEFICIT)	$	$	$

WHOLE-BAKED BUDGET

Whole-Baked Budget period ended   /   /

Goals We're Trying to Achieve:

	Actual	Budget	First Review
INCOME			
Salary/wages	$	$	$
Commissions/bonus			
Interest/dividends			
Business/partnership income			
Pensions			
Social Security			
Trust distributions			
Alimony/child support			
Sale of assets			
Gifts			
Tax refunds			
Other income			
Total Income	$	$	$
EXPENSES			
Savings	$	$	$
Goal #1			
Goal #2			
Goal #3			
Housing:			
Rent/mortgage			
Heat/light/water			
Telephone/cable			
Trash removal			
Maintenance			
Insurance			
Real estate taxes			
Improvements			

	Actual	Budget	First Review
Automobile:			
Loan payment			
Insurance			
Gas and oil			
Maintenance			
Commuting costs			
Laundry and cleaning			
Clothing purchases			
Furniture			
Medical/dental care and insurance			
Entertainment			
Dining out/takeout			
Groceries			
Personal care			
Business/professional expenses and allowances			
Child care expenses and allowances			
Tuition/educational expenses			
Child support and alimony			
Vacations			
Gifts			
Donations to church and charity			
Life/disability/other insurance			
Loan payments			
Credit card payments			
Income taxes			
Social Security taxes			
Miscellaneous out-of-pocket expenses			
Other (list):			
Total Expenses	$	$	$
CASH SURPLUS (DEFICIT)	$	$	$

CHAPTER 6: A PORTFOLIO BUILT FOR TWO
How Low Is Too Low (for your portfolio to go, that is)?

Answer the following three questions separately, and then discuss. Your answers will help you determine how much investment risk you're willing to take as a couple.

1. Which statement best describes your feelings about investing? (Circle one)

   a. I think the stock market is too risky.

   b. I'm comfortable investing in mutual funds.

   c. I believe the best place for our money is the stock market, with some of it in individual stocks.

   d. I'm always looking for the next big thing. "Risk" is my middle name. (Actually, "Rick" is my middle name, but I'm a rebel.)

2. I realize that every investment has its ups and downs, but we need to revisit any investment and make a decision about its future in our portfolio if it drops by _____ %. (Fill in the blank.)

3. A single stock should never make up more than _____ % of our total portfolio. (Fill in the blank.)

Now, couples, discuss. Then add a rule to your list of ground rules from Chapter 2 that communicates what you just discussed.

CHAPTER 7: WHAT YOUR HONEY *HAS* TO KNOW
Really Important Stuff Checklist

We'll forgive you if your eyes are glazing over by now. This stuff is a bit of a downer, and it takes a lot of time and effort to pull all this information together. Believe us, we wouldn't put you through this if it weren't *extremely* important. So please take the time now—you could be saving your partner a whole mess of trouble in the future.

Make copies of the following pages and store in a safe place.

Name: _____

Date of birth: _____

Social Security Number: _____

Bank Accounts
Safe-Deposit Box

Bank location: _____

Account number: _____

Documents stored there: _____

Who has access: _____

Checking Accounts

Bank name and phone number: _____

_____

Account number: _____

Account owner(s): _____

Bank name and phone number: _____

_____

Account number: _____

Account owner(s): _____

Savings Accounts

Bank name and phone number:_____
Account number:_____
Account owner(s): _____
Bank name and phone number:_____
Account number:_____
Account owner(s): _____

CDs and Money Market Accounts

Bank name and phone number:_____

_____

Account number:_____
Account owner(s): _____
Bank name and phone number:_____
Account number:_____
Account owner(s): _____

Investments
Brokerage Accounts

Bank/brokerage name and phone number: _____

_____

Account number:_____
Account owner(s): _____
Bank/brokerage name and phone number: _____
Account number:_____
Account owner(s): _____

IRA

Bank/brokerage name and phone number: _____

Account number:_____

Account owner:_____

Beneficiary:_____

Bank/brokerage name and phone number:_____

Account number:_____

Account owner:_____

Beneficiary:_____

401(k) or Other Pension Funds

Plan administrator and phone number:_____

Account number:_____

Account owner:_____

Beneficiary:_____

Plan administrator and phone number:_____

Account number:_____

Account owner:_____

Beneficiary:_____

Other Investments

Type of investment:_____

Location held and phone number:_____

Account number:_____

Account owner(s):_____

Type of investment:_____

Location held and phone number:_____

Account number:_____

Account owner(s): _____

Debts You Owe

Type of loan:_____

Lender name and address:_____

_____

Account number:_____

Amount of payment and due date:_____

Type of loan:_____

Lender name and address:_____

_____

Account number:_____

Amount of payment and due date:_____

Type of loan:_____

Lender name and address:_____

_____

Account number:_____

Amount of payment and due date:_____

Type of loan:_____

Lender name and address:_____

_____

Account number:_____

Amount of payment and due date:_____

Type of loan:_____

Lender name and address:_____

_____

Account number:_____

Amount of payment and due date:_____

Debts Others Owe You

Borrower's name, address, and telephone:_____

_____

Original loan balance and date borrowed:_____

_____

Annual interest rate charged: _____
Payment amount, frequency, and due date:_____

_____

Location of note or loan agreement:_____
Borrower's name, address, and telephone:_____

Original loan balance and date borrowed:_____

_____

Annual interest rate charged: _____
Payment amount, frequency, and due date: _____

_____

Location of note or loan agreement: _____

Insurance
Health Insurance
Plan administrator and phone number:_____

_____

Policy and group numbers:_____
Premium amount and due date:_____

Disability Insurance
Plan administrator and phone number:_____

_____

Policy and group numbers: _____
Premium amount and due date:_____

Life Insurance
Plan administrator and phone number:_____

_____

Account number:_____

Value (optional):_____

Premium amount and due date:_____

Plan administrator and phone number:_____

Account number:_____

Value (optional):_____

Premium amount and due date:_____

Other Insurance

Homeowners/renters insurance plan holder and policy
number: _____

Premium amount and due date:_____

Auto insurance plan holder and policy number:_____

Premium amount and due date:_____

Other insurance plan holders and policy numbers, premium amounts, and due dates:_____

_____

_____

_____

Documents
Legal Information

Make sure the following documents are updated to re-
flect your wishes. List the location of each below.

Property titles: _____

Durable power of attorney: _____

Medical care power of attorney:_____

Organ donor card:_____

Living will:_____

Last will and testament:_____

Other Documents
Birth certificate:_____
Marriage certificate:_____
Copies of income tax returns:_____
Business agreements (relating to corporations, partnerships, and sole proprietorships):_____

Funeral Arrangements
Use this space to write down any wishes you have regarding your funeral. If you have made arrangements already, list the name and address of the company and where to find the relevant documents.

_____
_____
_____
_____
_____
_____

Personal Advisers
Attorney's name, address, and phone number:

_____
_____
_____

Accountant's name, address, and phone number:

_____
_____
_____

Priest/minister/rabbi's name, address, and phone number:

_____

_____

_____

Primary physician's name, address, and phone number:

_____

_____

_____

Executor of your will's name, address, and phone number:

_____

_____

_____

Guardian for children's name, address, and phone number:

_____

_____

_____

Anyone else to be notified in the event of your death or
incapacity:

_____

_____

_____

_____

_____

_____

CHAPTER 8: MEETING PREP CHECKLIST

Task	Who	Done?
Schedule the meeting.		
Date:		
Time:		
Location:		
Reward:		
Make dinner reservations?		
Need a sitter?		
Aggressively guard the calendar slot.		
Find a briefcase or bag to hold summit resources.		
Make a photocopy of these worksheets. Put them in the bag.		
Find a calculator. Put it in the bag.		
Create a folder to hold meeting pages. Put it in the bag.		
Create a folder to hold past meeting pages. Put them in the bag.		
Gather basic insurance info:		
Life—Just coverage amounts		
Disability—Percent of salary replaced		
Find latest bank statement for emergency fund.		
Gather statements for all consumer debt showing amount owed and annual rate. Don't worry about mortgage or home equity loans.		
Credit cards		
Auto loans		
Student loans		
Other consumer debt, such as department store charge cards or other store credit.		
Most recent statements for all retirement savings accounts:		
401(k), 403(b), or SEP		
Company pensions, profit sharing		
Roth, traditional, or rollover IRAs		
Retirement annuities		
Other tax sheltered		
Other not tax-sheltered		

CHAPTER 8: PRACTICE MAKES PERFECT

Time to prepare for a financial summit with your spouse. Below you'll find a detailed agenda outlining the high points of your meeting.

Priority One: Prepare for Financial Emergencies

1. Review disability, life, and health insurance plans.
   - Does each of you know exactly what coverage the other has?

   - Even if you haven't completed all of your important papers from Chapter 7, can both of you at least find all relevant insurance documents?

   - Is your coverage sufficient to protect dependents (including each other) from financial Armageddon, should one of you become seriously injured or ill?

Disability Insurance

Q: Does each employed partner have disability insurance? (Circle one) Yes No

Possible action: We are not sure whether we have adequate disability insurance.

___(Initial here) agrees to do some research and present options by the next summit meeting.

Life Insurance

Let's start by taking stock. What is the total "death

benefit" for all in-force life insurance policies on each of you?

TOTAL LIFE INSURANCE COVERAGE	
Partner A	**Partner B**

Q: Are these totals balanced correctly? If one partner has a lot more income, chances are you'll have to replace a lot more income to maintain your current standard of living.

Q: Is everybody covered? If one partner doesn't draw a paycheck but provides critical dependent care or other services—services the other partner would have to pay to replace—then this "not working outside the home" partner should be covered, too.

Q: Do we have enough insurance? Typical rules of thumb range from three times to six times annual income as an appropriate coverage level (or three times to six times annual replacement costs for dependent care services). Are you in the right ballpark?

Of course, these are extremely rough estimates, and you might want to examine the topic more closely, especially given all the handy-dandy life insurance calculators on the Web these days. But we only have 90 minutes, here, so let's make some decisions:

Possible action: We are not sure whether we have adequate life insurance.

___(Initial here) agrees to do some research and present options by the next summit meeting.

Health Insurance

Health insurance is too complex a topic for a quick review summit, but let's ask a few important questions:

Q: Is everybody covered? Are there any new babies, other dependents, or suddenly unemployed partners? This cannot wait!

Possible action: Somebody we support is uninsured.

___(Initial here) agrees to do something about it tomorrow.

Q: If both partners are employed, have we ever compared health insurance plans across the two companies to find the best quality/cost tradeoff for covering us plus any dependents? Differences can be substantial and pay off more predictably than any stock research you might be doing!

Possible action: It's time to more carefully compare our health insurance plans to pick the best deal.

___(Initial here) agrees to do this before the next health insurance re-enrollment period for your current plan. S/he gets to spend (__) % of any annual savings on _____(Insert reward here).

2. Monitor the growth of your family "emergency fund." The goal here is liquid savings (*not* stocks or tax-sheltered retirement plans) equal to at least three to six months of regular household expenses.

Let's review:

Do we have a savings account, money market account, or money market brokerage fund investment with a well-defined portion specifically set aside as a three-months-living-expenses emergency fund?

Possible action:

___(Initial here) agrees to set up this clearly marked fund as soon as possible, even if just means opening up a passbook savings account with a minimum balance.

Q: Did we make at least $100 dollars worth of contributions to our emergency fund over the last three months?

Possible action: If not,

___(Initial here) will come up with a plan to get this taken care of as soon as it can reasonably be accomplished. Don't move on without this plan!

Q: What is the interest rate return of our emergency fund? Is the rate within a range of what brokerage money market funds (not bank money market accounts) are paying?

Possible action: We think we might be able to do much better in terms of emergency fund interest payments.

___(Initial here) would enjoy shopping for a better rate and presenting alternatives.

Priority Two: Make More Money Than You Spend

The second agenda topic is about easing your financial wagon toward the high road, gently but firmly. Ultimately, it all comes down to making more money than you spend on a regular basis.

Here's how to stick with that pledge:
1. **Review your total debt load.**
   Add up all consumer debt, including credit cards and automobile loans. Don't include your mortgage. Simply record the total amount owed and interest rate paid, by debt.

   Add up all the credit and loan balances and fill in the Grand Total. As you review, answer the following:

DEBTS (Ignore mortgage and home equity loans)

	Balance Owed	Interest Rate
Credit cards		
Auto loans		
Student loans		
Store charge cards or credit purchases		
Other		
Grand Total		N/A

Q: Is the Grand Total lower than it was at the last summit meeting?

Possible action: If our debt balance is not lower than at our last summit (if this is your first summit, you get a free pass on this one), we agree to slash spending over the next three months on (fill in three budget categories below):

A joint budget category (such as eating out together): _____

An individual budget category for Partner A:

_____

An individual budget category for Partner B:

_____

Q: Has the biggest dollar drop in balance, over the last three months, come from the highest interest rate debt?

Possible action: Over the next three months, we will focus on paying down our highest interest rate debt, which is _____ (enter highest rate debt item here).

Possible action: The structure of our mandatory loan payments prevents us from paying down our highest rate debt balance first.

___(Initial here) agrees to research options for refinancing or consolidating our debt so that we can attack the highest rate first.

2. Tally contributions to your retirement savings. Let's see how you're doing. Fill out the Retirement Savings Worksheet on the next page.

Add up all the retirement account contributions for the quarter and quarter-ending balances for each. Ready? Set? Review!

Q: Do any of our retirement plans offer employer-matching of your contributions? Have you taken full advantage of these immediate 25 percent or greater returns on investment? You sure won't beat these kinds of returns consistently in any stock market, even with superior investment options. Make it a priority to contribute enough of your paychecks, automatically, that you get the maximum company matching offered.

Possible action: We're not sure if we've maxed out our matching employer contributions.

___(Initial here) will investigate and fill out the necessary paperwork to increase our pre-tax payroll contributions accordingly.

Q: Overall, did we contribute roughly 6 percent or more of our total income for the quarter to our retirement savings?

Possible action: We'll set up automatic deductions from our paychecks—either to employer-

RETIREMENT SAVINGS

(Any account for which it's possible to obtain a current savings balance — excludes most pension plans)

	Quarterly Contributions	Balance
401(k), 403(b), SEP, or other employer-sponsored plans:		
Company profit-sharing or other defined contribution plan:		
Traditional, Roth, and rollover IRAs:		
Retirement annuities		
Other tax-sheltered:		
Other:		
Grand Total		

sponsored plans or to a brokerage IRA—to achieve this goal.

_____(Both partners initial here)

Possible action: There is no way that we can reach this 6 percent contribution rate in the short term.

___(Initial here) will come up with a budget cutting, debt pay down plan that will get us to this point as soon as possible.

Q: Has the investment rate of return on our retirement savings kept up with or surpassed the overall market rate, as represented by the S&P 500 over the past quarter?

Possible action: What's the S&P 500, dude?

___(Insert here) volunteers to reread Chapter 6 and report back on our performance versus the S&P 500.

Q: If you plan to make one or more $3,000 IRA deposits this year, are you on track with $750 in quarterly contributions? If you're on track for a $3,000 IRA contribution, the Roth IRA is the simpler and more flexible choice. If you are unable to come up with the full $3,000, though, a traditional IRA may boost your total contribution by allowing you to fund some of it with pre-tax dollars (practically speaking, from your tax return check).

3. Plan an additional savings goal.
In addition to your emergency fund and retirement, it helps to have at least one additional savings goal. If you're not sure how to arrive at this secondary savings goal together, maybe it's time to revisit Chapter 5. Whatever goal you choose, make it compelling enough to strengthen you both in moments of fiscal weakness.

Q: Can we agree on a significant, compelling savings goal that is shared by both of us?

Possible action: Our joint savings goal is listed below. We'll use it to motivate ourselves, and each other, to cut spending and pay down debt.

JOINT SAVINGS GOAL		
Goal	Amount	By This Date

Possible action: We're having a lot of trouble agreeing on a single joint goal.

___(Initial here) agrees to reread Chapter 4 about setting priorities and come up with a plan for agreeing on this joint goal.

Q: Can each of us come up with a personal savings goal (different from the joint goal) that will compel us to spend less and save more?

Possible action: Here are our personal savings goals:

PERSONAL SAVINGS GOAL		
Goal	**Amount**	**By This Date**
Partner A's compelling personal savings goal		
Partner B's compelling personal savings goal		

4. **Set the next date for your summit.** At a minimum, make a date to spend 90 minutes together once every three months.

Q: Have you marked on your calendar the date for your next summit meeting?

Possible action: Set the date. 'Nuff said.

Summary

You're in the home stretch now! If, in general, your debts are going down and your savings are going up, then congratulations! Stay the course.

If, in general, debt is getting bigger and savings are going nowhere, there's only one reason: You're spending all—or even more—than what you make on a regular basis. Unless you can come up with a way to markedly improve your income, you're going to have to cut some spending.

You've probably noticed that the word "budget" is missing from this recommended summit agenda. Ideally, of course, you'll follow some of what you learned earlier in this book and establish a budget. But, human nature and busy lives have a knack for undermining budgets. If this happens to you, at least you'll have these quarterly meetings to help track your progress. They won't tell you exactly where your money is going, but if you aren't making progress at the top level—if your total debt isn't getting smaller and your savings larger—then you know your current budget isn't working. Resolve to focus on these spending cuts as your top financial priority over the next three months. Cut something. Repeat until successful.

As we said before, it all comes down to making more money than you spend on a regular basis. This discipline is tough to develop overnight, though, and as you work your way toward it, it's a mistake to ignore the other half of the equation—emergency planning. Doing so could cost you, both financially and—perhaps more important to your life together—emotionally.

Index

Expenses
in budgeting, 114–115,
117–119
division of, 32
tracking, 52, 54–55, 59–60

F

Finances
changes in, over lifetime,
98–99
combining, 27–37
complexity of, 22
current state of, 21–38,
108–110
death and, 78
fixed assets in, 25
management of, and joint
accounts, 29–30
as nonissue, 100
Financial advice, paying for,
48
Financial decisions, types of,
x–xi
First Annual *Philadelphia
Inquirer* Cheapskate
Contest, 57
Fixed assets
examples of, 24
in financial planning, 25
Foolishness, definition of, iii
401(k)s
beneficiary designation on,
85
contributions to, 59, 70
current state of, 34–36
goals and, 45
record of, 123
Funeral arrangements, 83–84,
127

G

Goals
achieving, 48–49
arguments about, 47

budget and, 57
conversations about, 42–43,
45
in investing, 64–67
major, 43–45
priorities in, 44
in saving, 46–48, 98, 112–113
worksheet for, 111–113
Ground rules
in goal-setting, 47
for talking about money,
14–18, 106–107

H

Half-Baked Budget, 56, 117
Health insurance
record of, 125
reviewing, 36–37, 94–95,
132–133
Healthcare proxy
definition of, 83
location of, 126
remarriage and, 86
Honesty, 15–16
House. *See also* Mortgage
buying, 43
as fixed asset, 25
ownership of, 85
paying for, 48

I

Impulsive type, 4
Income
in budgeting, 114–118
discretionary, 52, 115
in merging finances, 32
vs. spending, 96–98
Independence
in budgeting, 59
joint accounts and, 30–33
Index funds, investing in, 70,
71–72
Insurance
current state of, 36–37

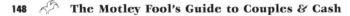

otley Fool

The Motley Fool's Guide to Paying for School: How to Cover Education Costs from K to Ph.D. by Robert Brokamp

The Motley Fool Investment Guide for Teens: Eight Steps to Having More Money Than Your Parents Ever Dreamed Of by David and Tom Gardner with Selena Maranjian

The Motley Fool Investment Workbook; Revised and Updated Edition by David and Tom Gardner

The Motley Fool Money Guide: Answers to Your Questions About Saving, Spending, and Investing by Selena Maranjian

The Motley Fool Personal Finance Workbook: A Foolproof Guide to Organizing Your Cash and Building Wealth by David and Tom Gardner with Robert Brokamp and Dayana Yochim

The Motley Fool's What To Do With Your Money Now: Ten Steps to Staying Up in a Down Market by David and Tom Gardner

The Motley Fool Investment Guide by David and Tom Gardner

The Motley Fool You Have More Than You Think by David and Tom Gardner